Tragedy and Denial

Tragedy and Denial

The Politics of Difference in Western Political Thought

Michael Brint

Westview Press
BOULDER • SAN FRANCISCO • OXFORD

All rights reserved. No part of this publication may be reproduced or transmitted in any form or by any means, electronic or mechanical, including photocopy, recording, or any information storage and retrieval system, without permission in writing from the publisher.

Copyright © 1991 by Westview Press, Inc.

Published in 1991 in the United States of America by Westview Press, Inc., 5500 Central Avenue, Boulder, Colorado 80301, and in the United Kingdom by Westview Press, 36 Lonsdale Road, Summertown, Oxford OX2 7EW

Library of Congress Cataloging-in-Publication Data
Brint, Michael.
  Tragedy and denial : the politics of difference in Western political thought / Michael Brint.
    p. cm.
  Includes bibliographical references and index.
  ISBN 0-8133-1225-6 — ISBN 0-8133-1226-4 (pbk.)
  1. Political science. 2. Tragic, The. I. Title.
JA74.B72 1991
320—dc20
                                                        91-8926
                                                           CIP

Printed and bound in the United States of America

The paper used in this publication meets the requirements of the American National Standard for Permanence of Paper for Printed Library Materials Z39.48-1984.

10   9   8   7   6   5   4   3   2   1

TO CAMILLE AND CASE

Contents

Acknowledgments   ix

Introduction   1

    Notes, 11

PART ONE
THE ANTITRAGIC THEATER
OF POLITICAL THOUGHT

1   **Happy Endings and Noble Lies in Plato's *Republic***   15

    A Note on Socrates' Death, 17
    The Trial of Poetry, 22
    Plato's Ironic Art, 26
    Happy Endings and Noble Lies, 30
    The Limits of Irony in Plato's *Republic*, 35
    Notes, 38

2   **Rousseau and the Echoes of *Narcisse***   41

    Phenomenology of the Theater, 44
    The Politics of Love and Estrangement, 48
    The Politics of Narcissism, 55
    Notes, 61

PART TWO
THE POLITICS OF TRAGEDY

3   **A Dialogue on Liberty and Freedom**   67

    Prologue: Inside Cervantes' Archives, 67
    The Battle of the Books, 70
    Constant on Ancient and Modern Liberty, 70
    Rousseau's Defense of Political Liberty, 78
    Notes, 84

| 4 | **Hegelian Harmony and the Laughter of Angels** | 87 |

Reconsidering the Conflict of Liberty and
  Freedom, 91
Hegel's Comic Ending to the Conflict, 100
The Laughter of Angels, 103
Notes, 107

| 5 | **A Carnival of Critics: Irony and the Postmodern Temper** | 109 |

Sartre's Satire, 112
Sartre's Satirical Ending to the Conflict, 114
From Satire to Self-Parody, 121
Notes, 127

| 6 | **Arendt, Rorty, and Mr. Jefferson's American Romance** | 131 |

Romance and the Romantics, 131
Hannah Arendt's Romance of the Past, 136
Richard Rorty's Romance of the Future, 143
Notes, 152

**PART THREE
CONCLUSION**

| 7 | **Putting the "E" Back into *Différance*** | 157 |

The Dialectics of Comedy, 158
The Ineffable Other, 161
A Different Kind of Otherness, 163
Notes, 167

Selected Bibliography — 169
About the Book and Author — 177
Index — 179

Acknowledgments

For their generous financial aid, I would like to express my gratitude to the University of Virginia Alumni Association, Summer Grants Program, and the Thomas Jefferson Memorial Foundation. I am also indebted to Spencer Carr, Cindy Hirschfeld, and Alice Colwell of Westview Press, whose competence, sensitivity, and intelligence proved invaluable in guiding this work to its final publication. To the kind editors of the *Review of Politics* and *Political Theory*, I am grateful for permission to republish parts of my essays on Rousseau. For their friendship, comments, and advice, I wish to thank David Thomas, Peter Euben, Jim Ceaser, Dante Germino, and Dick Rorty. To the many graduate and undergraduate students who have had to put up with my dramatic readings of political theory, I offer my sincere apologies and appreciation. In particular, my thanks go to Margaret Brabant, Reid Cushman, Meredith Garmon, Stuart Hall, Joseph Harder, David Hennigan, and Scott Roulier. In addition to his very helpful remarks, William Weaver also took on the task of preparing the manuscript for publication. Finally, and most importantly, for their laughter and love, I joyfully dedicate these essays to my wife, Camille, and to our son, Case Tyler.

Michael Brint
Charlottesville, Virginia

Introduction

It is appropriate for founders of political communities to know the models according to which the poets must tell their tales.
—Republic, 379a

The contours of our political culture are in large measure shaped by our diverse perceptions and understandings; by the ethical and political principles we invoke; by the rituals, customs, and ceremonies we observe; by the ways we explain and justify our actions; by the fundamental disagreements and conflicts we confront; and, not least, by the stories we tell about ourselves as a people. Some of the greatest stories ever told within and about our culture can be found, I shall argue, in the history of political thought.

But there is one kind of story that is too often neglected in this tradition. In telling their tales, political theorists have tended to ignore, evade, or cover up what A. C. Bradley once called the "essential fact" of tragedy. "It will be agreed," Bradley said, "that in all tragedy there is some sort of conflict—conflict of feelings, modes of thought, desires, wills, purposes; conflict of persons with one another, or with circumstances, or with themselves; one, several, or all of these kinds of conflict as the case may be."[1] The tragedy is that these conflicts are not so much wars of good with evil as they are wars of good with good.

At best, political theorists have tended to blink at such contests of values. Some simply refuse to recognize the existence of the clash between competing conceptions of the good. By logic or definition, they insist, the good cannot conflict with itself. But as long as our beliefs are contestable or corrigible, as long as we remain bound by the ethical indeterminacy of human life, we will find ourselves confronted by different and contending structures of belief, ways of life, spheres of cultural value, and moral descriptions of our social and political practices. To be forced to choose between two desirable, compelling, and justifiable but incompatible courses of action is an inexorable part of the repertoire of human experience.

Others, who acknowledge the existence of different conceptions of the good, argue that such goods can be calibrated or weighed through principle, procedure, priority rules, or community consensus. The metaphor of balancing goods is often used in these cases of adjudication. But if the values in question are distinct, then it is difficult to see what system of calibration or weight one can use to balance them. In fact, what is being balanced is not the different values in conflict but weights relative to some other standard into which these values have already been converted. In other words, the values in question in tragic conflicts are not different in relation to a presumed standard of weight and measure but in relation to each other. They constitute rival ways of describing our ethical and political actions. Because they are different, tragic conflicts defy such easy solutions as those predicated on a standard of conversion and evaluation.

Finally, throughout the Western political tradition, we find prescriptive schemes that are dedicated to banishing tragedy itself from the human domain. If we could but live in accord with the principles of unity, harmony, and synchronicity indicated, such thinkers contend, we could once and for all rid tragedy from the experience of human life. Although this desire to eliminate human tragedy might be described as the oldest and most noble goal of political thought, it could also be described as its most enduring failure. Such prescriptive schemes fail for the same basic reason the preceding descriptive proposals fail. They all deny the significance of relevant moral differences.

Rooted as tragedy is in the reality of human differences of values and interests, one simply cannot rid human life of it through philosophical presumption. To refuse to face this reality is a failure of political nerve. It is not merely that a world devoid of differences is a world that cannot be entertained in practice. Rather, the problem is that even if we could bring such a world into being, we would be

Introduction

better served by a world that endorsed and respected our ethical differences, even if by the very nature of these differences, we could not escape tragedy.

This book is dedicated to critically examining tragedy and its denial in the Western political tradition. In the first part of this work, I examine the denial of differences in the tales told by Plato and Rousseau. I begin with the complicated story of Plato's *Republic* as an antitragic narrative told in an ironic mode.[2] In less technical terms, I emphasize the ironic stance Plato takes in relation to the antitragic story he has Socrates tell. Concentrating on this ironic aspect of analysis, I offer a reading of the *Republic* as a text that simultaneously constructs and deconstructs itself, a story that both tells and untells itself. Before I more explicitly take up the themes of tragedy and antitragedy in relation to the *Republic*, let me say a few words about irony, a subtheme that will arise more than once in the pages that follow.

I must admit that I'm not convinced that irony, as both a mode of analysis and art, is all it's cracked up to be. Of course, I'm aware that ironic readings are extremely fashionable these days. And I appreciate irony's power as a theoretical tool or weapon. But as Germaine de Staël noted nearly two centuries ago, with its emphasis on ridicule, frivolity, surface play, and wit, irony is too skeptical, too doubtful, too disillusioned; in her words, it is just "too French."[3] Yet despite, or because of, its current appeal, many, especially those taken with deconstruction, neglect the limits of irony. For though it can subvert and disrupt the transparency of linguistic exchange upon which the West has built its "metaphysics of presence," irony does not open up new vistas.

Plato's *Republic* is a case in point. Although sometimes seen as the official founder and *bête noire* of Western metaphysics, Plato is clearly one of the great ironists in the Western tradition. Many have recognized the various levels of irony in Plato's *Republic*, but few have paid attention to its limits. On a narrative level, these limits are found in Plato's inability to escape from the endless cycle of repetition and denial inherent in the parasitic nature of his own satire. In challenging Socrates' vision, he employs his irony "without changing terrain, by repeating what is implicit in the founding concepts and the original problematic, by using against the edifice the instruments or stones available in the house, that is, equally, in language."[4] The problem, of course, is that by remaining on this terrain, Plato risks confirming and reaffirming that which he allegedly deconstructs. With the simultaneous yes and no of the ironic mode, with its repetition of that which it denies, Plato can never free himself from the language of Socrates' city of words. As parasite, he must raise Socrates' city only to raze it in an endless play of irony.

Socrates' antitragic art can best be understood in contradistinction to three themes commonly associated with classical drama. First, tragic compositions tend to focus on the theme of human vulnerability, specifically on the vulnerability of human life to the contingent forces of moral luck (*tyche*) or misfortune. Indeed, Aristotle described the movement from fortune to misfortune as a theme typical of the peripety of a complex tragic plot. In contrast, the antitragic vision articulated in Socrates' city of words is founded on the possibility of overcoming the contingencies of political life and human happiness.[5]

In addition to its quest for invulnerability, Socrates' antitragic vision is predicated on his demands for linguistic purity and transparency. Indeed, such transparency of linguistic exchange is elemental to Socrates' quest for understanding what justice itself is. This brings us to our second contrast between Socrates and tragic drama: Tragic compositions are often characterized by their linguistic opacity and lexical ambiguity (*homōnumia*).[6] Rather than attempting to find the univocal meaning of such terms as *justice*, tragic narratives urge us to distinguish among the various semantic fields (religious, juridical, and military) within which the discursive practice of justice is considered appropriate.

Finally, as we have already witnessed, in what is perhaps its most prominent theme, classical tragedy often portrays the collision between distinct spheres of cultural value and ethical practice. For example, the value placed on kinship ties is often portrayed in conflict with the value garnered in the name of the city and its honor. This conflict is traditionally conceived in terms of gender differences.

Introduction

Socrates, on the other hand, attempts to resolve this human tragedy on the basis of his principle of specialization. By defining one's excellence (*aretē*) in terms of one's nature (*physis*), he radically transforms the values conventionally associated with the genders in both Homeric and classical texts. Gender, he argues, is simply not relevant to the realization of one's natural excellence in terms of one's capacity to fulfill the function of guardianship. The integrity of moral principle necessary for this function is a matter of an individual's character and soul, he claims, not of one's physical constitution or gender.

Although I agree that excellence is not gendered, Socrates nevertheless conflates, condenses, and reduces the complex functions that, with equal (but not necessarily the same) excellence, human beings perform in ethical life. According to his principle of specialization, each person ought to perform the single function for which he or she is, by nature, best suited. On the surface, Socrates thus appears to be emphasizing the significance of different, specialized contributions to his city. But he sharply limits the repertoire of these differences in his community of guardians by offering us a single integrative vision without inner differentiation. The guardians are to make no distinction between the family and the polis. Indeed, they are to conceive of themselves as one big happy family. In this way, Socrates' vision of community is a whole bound together by a suspiciously simple principle of unity. Of course, there is more than an obvious loss of functional complexity in this model. Socrates fundamentally eliminates the significance of various kinds of differences, differences in the spheres of our activity, differences in our ethical voices, and differences in our ways of life.

In important respects, Jean-Jacques Rousseau mirrors Socrates' antitragic narrative. In the second chapter, I examine Rousseau's first written work, *Narcisse*, a sexual comedy about a man who falls in love with a portrait of himself dressed as a woman. Throughout his life, Rousseau was clearly obsessed by the problem of narcissism. "Always outside ourselves," he complained, "we draw the very sentiment of our existence from how we are perceived and judged by others."[7] For Rousseau, narcissism is really a problem of self-estrangement. We become obsessed with ourselves only when we become objects of consciousness for others. In attempting to overcome this problem in his political thought, Rousseau offers us a vision of a political community, not unlike Socrates' *callipolis*, that banishes differences and eliminates from the purity of its vision the significance and value of contending ethical views.

To my mind, it is not the differences in our principles or the plurality of our voices but the desire for such ethical unity that is both morally questionable and culturally incoherent. Indeed, no significant or challenging moral debates are possible in such unitary cultural communities. Moral judgment is rendered by the imposition of one ethical voice or way of life (with its internal rational standards and principles) over the many. The result is that contending voices must be silenced, expropriated, or eliminated.

Moreover, those who endorse antitragic schemes of unity fail to recognize that different ethical positions need rival ways to bound off against or ally with for their own definition and distinction. Without such differences, narcissistic schemes of unity collapse in on themselves. In this respect, it is not the conflict of values associated with ethical pluralism but the antitragic elements contained in Rousseau's civic community that are theoretically incoherent.

Having considered the themes of antitragic unity in the first two chapters, I take up the problem of tragic conflict more explicitly in the next part of this work. I begin with a story told by Cervantes. In part 1 chapter 9 of the *Adventures of Don Quixote*, we find the valiant Quixote embattled with a gallant Basque. Just as these two mortal enemies are about to seal each other's fate, Cervantes leaves the text in search of an ending. Following Cervantes, I too recount a story of a battle suspended. One of the most vexing problems in most modern Western polities is, of course, the tension between what are often called "liberal" and "republican" conceptions of liberty and freedom. On one side lies our desire for individual free agency, our liberty to define our lives and ends without interference by others. On the other side lies our demand for democratic self-rule earned through civic duty and public participation. Poised between the

Introduction

ethical forces we respectively place on these contending conceptions, I leave us temporarily suspended.

In the next three chapters, I offer three different stories political theorists have traditionally told in coming to terms with the relation between individual liberty and political freedom. "The Laughter of Angels" contains Hegel's comic approach to this tragic conflict, "A Carnival of Critics" examines the satiric and parodic elements inscribed in the works of Jean-Paul Sartre and Jacques Derrida, and "Mr. Jefferson's American Romance" explores the respective romantic tales offered by Richard Rorty and Hannah Arendt.

In contrast to the antitragic themes of Socrates and Rousseau, Hegel's "comic" narrative does not seek to eliminate the "source" of ethical conflict. For instance, whereas Socrates conflates the family and the polis, Hegel preserves these differences while attempting to overcome any tension between them. Indeed, he insists that all tragic conflicts must find their source of unity in the affirmation that emerges through the "negation of the negation." In his ending to the conflict of liberty and freedom, he employs this narrative grammar to articulate and codify the political goals of unification.

In his terms, the state accomplishes the unity of freedom and liberty in its universality and in its particularity. While in civil society individuals have the capacity to define themselves and their ends without interference by others; in relation to the state, they identify with the universal will of all. Thus uniting the desire for individual liberty with the universal demands of freedom, Hegel's comedy can be understood as a tragedy that ends happily.

Yet one is apt to wonder whether Hegel's vision of unification, like irony, is all it's made out to be. For some, as we will see, his portrayal of the "universal will of the state" appears as little more than a veil for particularity, for the particular interests and aims of the monarch, the bureaucrats, and the estates. In this way, Hegel's "universality" conceals the fundamental contradictions that continue to exist both between *l'homme et le citoyen* on an individual level and between the interests of civil society and those of the state on an institutional level. In contrast, others claim that given the privileged status of the state, the universal will subsumes and ultimately undermines the value of individual liberty.

Finally, many postmodern thinkers have attacked Hegel's comic vision, his highly contentious claim that a political culture's moral requirements and principles can ultimately be unified into a harmonious whole through the logic of dialectical sublation. Against his appropriative schemes, they pose the ineffable Other as that which neither yearns for nor yields to but satirically ruptures dialectical sublation. For them, the Other stands outside the grasp of the Hegelian system's claim that every Other is a negation of itself; something that can be brought back within the presence of itself. In contrast, the Other must always be something mythical or mystical. Indeed, the only thing we can say about the Other is that we can't grasp it: The Other is the unspeakable. It is that which is systematically excluded from Hegel's comic vision. Lying beyond the system and its narrative grammar, the Other poses a challenge to Hegel's dialectical yearning to overcome cultural conflict through a politics of sublation.

In exploiting the internal logic of Hegel's system, such satirical tales seem, by their very nature, to be subversive and critical. The claim that they provide new vistas and constructive possibilities by breaking the tablets of our cultural inscriptions is largely a chimera. Rather than offering a constructive vision of their own, they endlessly repeat that which they deny. Consider, for instance, Sartre's "Republic of Silence."

As an act of resistance, Sartre tells us, freedom itself is founded in silence; it is established "in shadows and in blood."[8] Defined in opposition to oppression, his voice of liberation cannot and does not pretend to integrate the goals of democratic freedom with the principles of individual liberty. Rather, he expresses the idea of liberation as the desire for purity and totality in a world where oppression is said to end. He speaks of purity as an act of total responsibility in total solitude and of totality itself as the desire to become God. And yet, as satirical, this vision is cast only to be shattered by the force of its own impossibility. In this way, Sartre affirms only to deny our aspirations for happy endings and noble lies.

Not unlike Plato's ironic dialogue, the idea of linguistic transparency is thus momentarily resurrected only to be dissolved once again in an endless play of *différance*. As the gap and distance inherent in all speech acts, *différance* is said to inhabit the opaque terrain of what appears to be immediate and present. The illusion of the self-presence of meaning or of consciousness is thus presumed an impossibility, a façade and mask covering over *différance*. In this respect, Derrida's deconstructive efforts may best be described as an attempt to demonstrate the suppression of *différance* as the basis of all claims to Being and Presence, claims that are predicated on an implicit hierarchy and suppression of the Other. By giving voice to the Other, Derrida's satire is meant to disrupt the transparent presence of being. But, as Derrida himself knows, the parasitism inherent in such satire is bound to a dialectic of identity and alterity from which it cannot escape. Giving voice to the Other simply reverses the poles so that the tainted becomes the pure and the pure becomes tainted.

Rather than repeating the claims for transparency and purity found in comic and satirical works, Richard Rorty radically transposes the tasks of philosophy. If like Rorty, one does not put much faith in the language of "presence," "representation," and "transparency," then one need not feel particularly threatened by the parasitism of words that are presumed to eat away at the foundations of linguistic purity. Indeed, if one accepts the contingency of language, as Rorty does, then one should just drop the idea that language is foundational.

Philosophy "falls into self-deception," he tells us, "whenever it tries to do more than send the conversation off in new directions."[9] Indeed, the point of philosophy is "to perform the social function of preventing man from deluding himself with the notion that he knows himself, or anything else, except under optional descriptions."[10] In his view, philosophy's critical task is therapeutic: It forces us to recognize our self-delusions; it breaks what John Dewey called "the crust of convention." Leaving this ground broken, Rorty builds a philosophy without foundations.

Like Dewey, Rorty offers us a romance of the future. The United States' never-ending, open possibilities of novel events, experiences, and social structures, Dewey wrote, "facilitated the birth of a philosophy which regards the world as being in continuous formation, where there is still place for indeterminism, for the new and for a real future."[11] Unlike the Old World, burdened by an inherited stock of old ideas, prejudices, and metaphors, this new philosophy of pragmatism was dedicated to constructing the multivalent possibilities of this real future.

In contrast to Rorty's pragmatic romance of the future, romantics like Hannah Arendt tend to be interested in the process of reviving, revitalizing, and reinterpreting the lessons and metaphors of the past as a way of challenging present conditions. In this respect, there is a tone of both elegy and urgency to their message. Rather than simply lamenting the ineluctable loss of a better way of viewing and acting in the world, like Rorty's own romance, these tales serve therapeutic and edifying functions.

By reawakening our understanding of the metaphors and stories of the past, such romances at once criticize the often barren and ossified language of prevailing political practices and offer radical possibilities for political and social transformation. Instead of urging a return to halcyon days, they thus perform the edifying task of creative anachronism, of urging the radical transformation of our political practices to reflect the ideals we have lost.

In important respects Rorty's romance of the future and Arendt's romance of the past are less mutually exclusive alternatives than mirrored theoretical doubles. For Arendt, as we will see, the political realm of democratic freedom must be privileged over other domains and activities because it is within this realm that decisions are made about who we are and what we value. Arguing against all such privileged acts, Rorty valorizes individual liberty in order to secure the individual from the maleficent effects of cruelty and domination that have historically been imposed in the name of our most cherished projects of freedom and autonomy.

Where the one-sided romances of Rorty and Arendt meet their limits, we find the theoretical strengths of such tragic compositions as those offered by Sophocles. In the concluding chapter, I tell the tale of the *Antigone* three times. *Antigone* is often understood as a tragic confrontation with the Other, a term almost as fashionable and oblique as irony. As a first step in clarifying the semantic field of Otherness, I analyze the relation between Creon and Antigone as a conflict among the dialectical, the ineffable, and the different. Arguing that the first two characterizations of the Other (associated with Hegel and Derrida respectively) are inadequate, I end by urging that we put the "e" back into *différance*. In less circumlocutory terms, I urge a respect for our ethical differences in coming to terms with the conflicts, contingency, and opacity that inevitably result from the complex and diverse principles, traditions, rituals, ways of life, and stories that we tell about ourselves as a people.

Notes

1. A. C. Bradley, *Oxford Lectures on Poetry* (Oxford: Oxford University Press, 1950), 70.

2. On the distinction between genre and mode, see Alastair Fowler, *Kinds of Literature* (Cambridge, Mass.: Harvard University Press, 1982), 106-130. The narratives contained within the history of political thought are not simply literary embellishments that can be jettisoned without loss. Rather, they are components of a very complicated language game. As a communicative practice, the narrative grammar of a text collocates and arranges the interconnection of arguments, concepts, facts, and logic so as to heighten the dramatic effect of the whole. In turn, the narrative composition of the whole expresses the political arguments and vision of a text. It is the kind of story a political theorist tells in representing and reconstituting political life.

3. Germaine de Staël, *De l'allemagne*, ed. Jean de Pange (Paris: Librairie Hachette, 1959), tome 4, 64.

4. Jacques Derrida, "Les Fins de l'homme," in *Marges de la philosophie* (Paris: Editions de Minuit, 1972), 162. Unless otherwise indicated, all translations in the book are my own.

5. See Martha Nussbaum's nonironic reading of the *Republic* in *The Fragility of Goodness* (Cambridge: Cambridge University Press, 1986).

6. On this point, see Jean-Pierre Vernant's essays, "Tensions et ambiguïtés dans la tragédie grecque," and "Ambiguïté et renversement. Sur la structure énigmatique d'*Oedipe-Roi*," in Jean-Pierre Vernant and Pierre

Vidal-Naquet, *Mythe et tragédie en grèce ancienne* (Paris: Maspero: 1972), 19-49, 99-133.

7. Jean-Jacques Rousseau, *Discours sur l'origine et les fondements de l'inégalité* in *Oeuvres complètes*, ed. Bernard Gagnebin and Marcel Raymond (Paris: Gallimard, 1964), tome 3, 193.

8. Jean-Paul Sartre, "La République du Silence," in *Situations 3* (Paris: Gallimard, 1949), 14.

9. Richard Rorty, *Philosophy and the Mirror of Nature* (Princeton, N.J.: Princeton University Press, 1979), 378.

10. Ibid., 379.

11. John Dewey, "The Development of American Pragmatism," in *John Dewey, The Later Works 1925-1953*, ed. Jo Ann Boydston (Carbondale, Il.: Southern Illinois University Press, 1984), vol. 2, 19.

PART ONE

The Antitragic Theater of Political Thought

1

Happy Endings and Noble Lies in Plato's *Republic*

Inscribed in book 7 of the *Laws* are the final words Plato was to write on poetry and the arts. There, like Socrates before him, he has the Athenian stranger perform the ritual of banishing the poets from his imaginary city. In condemning the poets, Plato's protagonist seems to go out of his way to remind us that his city is itself a poetic construction that cannot allow other poetic visions to enter its imaginary gates. Both for its ironic candor and for its definition of "true" tragedy, this well-known passage bears repeating:

> As for our tragic poets, and their so-called serious compositions, suppose that some of them were to approach us and question us in terms similar to these: "Strangers, would you allow us to frequent your city and your territory, and could we bring with us our poetry to perform?" Now what would be an appropriate response to give to such inspired men? If I'm not mistaken, this should be our reply: "Best among strangers, we too, in measure with our ability, are authors of a tragedy, the best and most beautiful we know how to make. In fact, our whole polity has been constructed as a representation of the noble and perfect life; that is what we affirm to be in truth the most real of tragedies. Thus you are poets and we too are poets in the same style, rival artists and rival actors, and that in the fairest drama of all. . . . So don't go and imagine that we shall lightly allow you to set up your stage next to ours in the market-place with a troupe of im-

ported actors whose dulcet voices will drown our own, and let you deliver your public tirades before . . . our women and children and the populace as a whole—let you address them on the same issues as ourselves, not to the same effect, but for the most part to the very opposite. Why, we would be absolutely mad to do so. (*Laws* 817a-c)[1]

For Plato, true tragedy always ends happily. As a drama of the good and noble life, it portrays a realm where ethical conflicts are overcome, where linguistic transparency reigns, and where human happiness is said to be invulnerable to the contingency and misfortunes of life. In this respect, Plato's true tragedy is undoubtedly antitragic. Against the opacity, contingency, and conflicts of cultural life that tragedy heaves to the surface, Plato offers us the confident verities of linguistic clarity, the invulnerable goods of the intellect, and the prospects for cultural and political harmony.

In depicting this antitragic drama in the *Republic*, Plato represents Socrates representing the good and noble life.[2] Of course, there is no small irony in this depiction. Plato situates his own narrative voice three removes from the kingdom of truth, in the position notoriously reserved for the poets Socrates banishes. Indeed, drawing from the arsenal of classical drama itself, Plato deconstructs the very vision he has Socrates construct.

At the end of the *Symposium*, Socrates claims that "he who knows how to produce tragedy by art would also know how to produce comedy" (223d). In his deconstruction, Plato deploys an ironic use of both tragic and comic themes to challenge Socrates' poetic construction of the good and noble life. Through wordplay, puns, and jokes, he employs comic tactics to subvert Socrates' vision of harmony and political unity. Reintroducing the themes of opacity, conflict, and vulnerability, he also uses tragic effects to undermine Socrates' antitragic story. In this way, though the true tragedy of Socrates' antidrama always ends happily, we will see that the happy endings in Plato's dialogues are never more, but often less, than noble lies.

A Note on Socrates' Death

Throughout the middle dialogues, Socrates' life is portrayed as ending happily. For example, note Socrates' own comparison with Achilleus in the *Apology*: "You are mistaken, my friend," Socrates says, "if you think that a man who is good for anything ought to spend his time calculating the prospects of life and death. According to your argument, the great heroes who died at Troy would be poor creatures, particularly the son of Thetis." Indeed, it will be recalled, Socrates goes on to say,

> that he made light of danger in comparison with enduring dishonor when his goddess mother warned him in words such as these, if I'm not mistaken: "Son, if you avenge the death of your comrade Patroklos by slaying Hektor, eager as you are to do so, you will yourself die. After Hektor, thine own death is prepared." When he heard this warning, he made light of his death and peril, being much more afraid of leading an ignoble life (28c-d).

As any Athenian would know, the *Iliad* suggests that Achilleus does not view his own death in quite this light. Rather, his mother, Thetis, warns Achilleus of his fate well before the death of Patroklos. Indeed, his friend's death itself is a consequence of Achilleus' tragic fate. Mirroring the structure of opposition so frequently detailed in the works of tragedy, in Book 9 of the *Iliad*, Achilleus recollects the incompatible destinies that lie before him:

> Of possessions cattle and fat sheep are things to be had for the lifting, and tripods can be won, and the tawny highheads of horses, but a man's life cannot come back again, it cannot be lifted nor captured again by force, once it has crossed the teeth's barrier. For my mother Thetis the goddess of the silver feet tells me I carry two sorts of destiny toward the day of my death. Either, if I stay here and fight beside the city of the Trojans, my

return home is gone, but my glory shall be everlasting; but if I return home to the beloved land of my fathers, the excellence of my glory is gone, but there will be a long life left for me, and my end in death will not come to me quickly.[3]

Either leave the battle of Troy to live a long and prosperous life without honor, or, inevitably die the death of a noble warrior: Reflecting on his fate, Achilleus is anything but desperate to reenter the battle. Indeed, on first reflection he urges his fellow Argives to leave Ilion. Unwilling to take this step, however, he then tries to elude his fate by allowing Patroklos to return to the Achaians vested in Achilleus' image, wearing his armor as a symbolic representation of himself. It is only when his comrade-in-arms dies that Achilleus, in a fit of madness (*atē*) and desire for revenge, pursues his own death both literally and figuratively by chasing and finally defeating Hektor who, having killed Patroklos, is in turn wearing Achilleus' armor.

The element of tragedy, the collision of fate, contained within the structure of the story of Achilleus' death obviously does not commend Socrates' reading of Achilleus as a man who simply "mocked life in the face of death." Here, Socrates is, no doubt, consciously transforming the Homeric understanding of the heroic ethos. He is, for instance, implicitly criticizing the idea that one's true honor is won or lost on the field of battle. Indeed, from Athenian experience, Socrates knew only too well that one tends to lose one's humanity well before one's honor in war. He is also rejecting the idea that honor can properly be bestowed in terms of how one is perceived by others in relation to a conventional standard of excellence (*aretē*). True excellence is said to be neither predicated on perception nor dependent on conventional recognition. Finally, and most importantly for our present purpose, Plato depicts Socrates' as replacing Achilleus' tragic vision of life with his own "truly tragic" attitude toward death.

In the *Phaedo*, for example, this transformation is evident in Socrates' articulation of the belief that death is a form of liberation, a remedy to life, and a flight into illumination. He tells us,

> A man who has really devoted his life to philosophy should be cheerful in the face of death, and assured of finding the greatest blessings in the next world. Other people seem not to realize that those who pursue philosophy in its proper sense are directly and of their own accord preparing themselves for dying and death. If this is true, it would be absurd to be troubled when that for which they have been eagerly practicing finally comes. (*Phaedo*, 64a)

Socrates' remarks are immediately made into a joke: "Simmias laughed [*gelasas*] and said, By God, Socrates, I don't feel much like laughing [*gel-*], but you made me laugh [*gel-*]. I am sure that if they heard what you said, most people at home would think that it was a very good crack at philosophers to say that they are half dead already" (64b).[4] The triple repetition of laughter in the first line echoes a traditional Greek understanding of the division between comedy and tragedy in terms of the *geleoin* (the low and laughable) and the *spoudaion* (the elevated and serious).

From Simmias' perspective, Socrates' vertical ascent (*anabasis*) to a realm invulnerable to the misfortunes and contingency of fate appears devoid of those attachments to life that are recognizably human—after all, philosophers are half dead already. For a brief moment, Simmias draws us back to the human domain. In contrast to Socrates' search for a stable, pure, and true world, he reminds us that we inhabit a world bounded by our own all-too-human physicality, finitude, grief, and laughter.

From the elevated perspective of the philosopher, however, death constitutes a happy ending to life. The soul is transported into the realm of the infinite, leaving far behind it the finite and contradictory world of (what Dante would surely describe as the inferno of) existent reality. As Socrates reports: "The soul passes into the realm of the pure and everlasting and immortal and never changing; and being of a kindred nature, it dwells unhindered in this realm of the absolute, constant, and invariable" (79d).

In his arguments for the immortality of the soul, Socrates raises his famous doctrine of knowledge as recollection (*anamnēsis*). In substantiating the unity of the soul in its immortality, he claims that true knowledge, the knowledge of the absolute, can be brought to light only through the recollection of the soul's immortality. The source of the knowledge of the ultimate unity of the world can be unveiled only by the soul's recollection of its immortal flight. This idea of recollecting one's own immortality as the basis of true knowledge is a rather persistent theme in Plato's dialogues, found, for example, not only in the *Phaedo* and *Meno* but throughout the *Republic* as well.

For instance, the familiar patterns of death and knowledge are given figurative shape in the narrative structure of Plato's allegory of the cave. Only after the ascent (*anabasis*) to the eternal is the prisoner in a position for recollection and knowledge. "If he recalled [*anamimnē-*] to mind his first habitation and what passed for wisdom there," Socrates tells us, the prisoner would now see with clarity and perspicuity the illusions he harbored in his former life among the shadows.

On a structural level, the linearity of his navigational ascent has its temporal analogue in his experience of death as life's journey to the eternal. Indeed, the prisoner could only resolve the irony inherent in seeing his former life as a mere semblance of reality by escaping from the finitude of his condition and viewing his past from a position outside the barriers of mortality. In this way, the prisoner's ironic predicament is allegorically resolved by finding a point of closure in time that nevertheless resides outside the finite condition of his former life.[5] This point of closure is, of course, a figure of death.

The survival of the prisoner's own death and its recollection thus constitutes the narrative perspective from which he views his former life. With these recollections in mind, the prisoner makes the descent (*katabasis*) back to the cave in order to instruct others regarding the proper ordering of the soul. The paideutic lessons he attempts to teach once again lead, however, only to laughter (*gel-*) and ultimately to the literal death of the prisoner, whose identity then merges with that of Socrates.

This same pattern is much more explicitly repeated in the final images of the *Republic*. In the myth of Pamphylian, Er, Socrates depicts the story of a man who, having survived his own death, recollects the knowledge he gained in "the world beyond." In his recollections of the eternal, Er tells the story of the soul's choices when confronting its fate. Reflecting on this myth, Socrates remarks, "it will save us, if we let ourselves be persuaded by it" (621c).

It has often been claimed that Plato substitutes Socrates for Er.[6] The *Republic* might then be seen as a story of a man who, surviving his own death, descends to tell the tale of his immortal flight. Such a tale will save us, Plato seems to suggest, if only we are persuaded by it. To punctuate this point, the *Republic* begins with the word *kateben* (I went down). In conventional usage, *katabasis* refers to a descent into the underworld in search of understanding. Note, for example, Homer's famous use of the term: "I went down [*kateben*] to Hades," Odysseus tells Penelope, "to inquire about the return of myself and my comrades and there learned of the measureless toil that still was in store for me to fulfill to the end" (*Odyssey* 23, 252).

Although *kateben*, may well announce the theme of death in the *Republic*, there appears to be a complication in Plato's deployment. Homer's Hades seems to be symbolically linked to the Piraeus of the *Republic*. "I went down to the Piraeus," Socrates begins, "to pray to the goddess and see how her festival was to be organized" (327a). Bendis, the goddess to whom Socrates refers, is undoubtedly associated with the chthonic Hecate who attends the souls on the way to the underworld. But, from Plato's perspective, the Piraeus itself was seen as the seat of the radical *dēmos*, a center of commercial activity and a home for luxury and unconstrained passion. Rather than a place of knowledge ruled in accordance with the divine, it appears to be an example of what Socrates might call a "city of unjust souls."

If Homeric Hades is associated with the Piraeus, then the *katabasis* appears asymmetric to the ascent of the prisoner in the cave allegory. But, a detail in the myth of Er may help provide a clue to this asymmetry. When the soul of the Pamphylian went forth from his body, Socrates says,

> he journeyed . . . to a mysterious region where there were two openings side by side in the earth, and above and over against

them in the heaven two others. Between these, judges were sitting. After every judgment, they commanded the righteous to journey to the right and upwards through the heavens . . . and the unjust to take the path to the left and downward. (614c)

Here, the directional indication that the souls of the just ascend while those of the unjust descend once again inverts the traditional use of *katabasis*. However, this inversion becomes somewhat clearer when we realize that by linking the Piraeus with Homer's Hades, Socrates appears to be employing a kind of infernal irony: Homer's Hades is meant to signify the city of unjust souls—the Piraeus. On the other hand, Socrates' own use of *kateben* (I went down) appears to indicate his descent from the heavens. In this way, *katabasis* is ironically linked to both experiences of descent.

This point may be further substantiated by the directional inversion found in Plato's *Timaeus*. There, such inversion is explicitly related to the soul's *paideia*. Indeed, the symptom of the soul's disorder is given figurative expression in the disruption of what Timaeus calls the circles of reason and passion in the soul. For such disordered souls, it is as if a "man were standing on his head, resting it on the earth, and holding his feet aloft against something above him: in such a case right and left both of the man and of the spectators appear reversed to the other party" (43e).

The Trial of Poetry

Within the inverted world of Socrates' city of words, it is not the philosopher but the poets who are put on trial. As in the case of Socrates, the charges are impiety and corrupting the youth. And, just as Socrates was condemned for "not minding his own business," so the poets will be seen as transgressing the proper bounds of justice. The punishment under the laws of the world of appearance that disgrace and dishonor Socrates are thereby transformed in the inverted world into the disgrace and dishonor of those who condemned him. Hence, consummate with Plato's logic of inversion, what in the former world was honored, in Socrates' city meets only with contempt.

Socrates' trial of poetry takes place within the context of discussing the proper education of the guardians of his city. Unlike his later attacks against the ontological and epistemological elements of art, Socrates is here interested in establishing a model and pattern of action and thought for the young as a first step in creating the proper ordering of their souls. This enterprise is clearly directed against Homer and the poets who were traditionally considered the "educators of Greece." In contrast to such traditional wisdom, Socrates claims that in the stories they tell, poets like Homer invert the proper ordering of the soul. Indeed, from the perspective of Socrates' inverted world, Homer appears to see the world both upside down and distorted. In order to set the world aright, Socrates seems to suggest, our own cultural horizons must be inverted.

In general terms, the idea of a cultural horizon of knowledge signifies the way in which our linguistic and cultural practices frame and structure our imagination and perceptions of reality. It is closely connected to what Jean-Pierre Vernant has called "the structure of social thought" or what Michel Foucault has termed our "discursive practice": the way in which we structure and organize our understanding of the order of things and our place within that order.[7] It should not be surprising to find that this idea does not begin with Friedrich Nietzsche, but with his self-proclaimed arch-nemesis. As Plato depicts him, Socrates clearly believes that our perceptions of reality and identity are framed and shaped by the stories we tell about ourselves. Indeed, given his own *callipolis*, he obviously endorses the mytho-poetic power of cultural narratives both in their capacity for world-building and in their ability to shape the very souls of the young. His recognition of the mytho-poetic power of traditional stories is indicated by the first argument leveled against the poets in the second book of the *Republic*.

Charging that the poets have corrupted the youth through the stories they tell, Socrates claims that the young are extremely impressionable. Their souls can be easily shaped and molded by the stories they hear. Indeed, these stories not only structure the imagination of the youth but construct the cognitive and linguistic fields within which they come to comprehend their experiences in the world. For this reason, the first task in determining the proper education of the young is "to strictly supervise the storytellers and separate those who produce true stories from those who produce false ones. We'll induce mothers and nurses to tell the acceptable stories to their children to shape their souls with them even more than their bodies with their hands" (377a-c). The implication of Socrates' remark is that whereas traditional poetry disfigures the souls of the young, his own divine art will "stamp on their souls" the impression of excellence that accords to their nature.[8]

Turning to the second indictment, Socrates maintains that the most serious form of corruption inspired by the poetry of Homer and the tragedians is contained in the stories they tell of the divine. Recall that in the very first line of the *Republic*, Homer's Hades was linked to the Piraeus. Following the logic of symbolic inversion implicit in this connection, Homer and the poets appear to embrace an "infernal" view of the divine. Of course, I do not mean that they embody a Christian conception of sin. Rather, I mean that they perceive reality and divinity from the inverted perspective of the Piraeus. From this view, Socrates warns, the poets ascribe laughter to that which is truly worthy and divine; they reverse the fields of the *geleoin* and *spoudaion*. Inverting such poetic inversion, Socrates claims, those who are "seriously inclined to listen to such tales" should be taught to "laugh at them as unworthy utterances" (388d).

For instance, consider the inversion of the *geleoin* and *spoudaion* in book 2 where Glaucon laughingly calls Socrates' first "true city" of words a city of swine. Although leveled against Socrates, the joke is actually on Glaucon. He figuratively perceives the "true" city from the point of view of a sow. The object of ridicule is made abundantly clear when Socrates adopts Glaucon's suggestion that luxury should be introduced into the city. The effect is, of course, that Socrates thereby creates a city of swine. Through a beautiful dialectical move, Socrates then introduces the guardians who will ultimately banish the swine from the city. On a paideutic level, the point is that Glaucon must banish his own swine-like desires from his soul. If he initially saw the world from the perspective of these desires, he must now learn to view it from more divine heights. In this way, the ironic play of desires (true vs. swinelike) mirrors the inversion which Glaucon's soul must undertake.

The implications of this inverted perspective are further explored when Socrates takes up the epistemological problems of art in book 10. There he transforms the language of inversion into a rhetoric of distance. On a vertical axis of knowledge reminiscent of his divided line, Socrates claims that the position of his own divine perspective is three removes from the inverted perspective of the artist. In other words, Socrates sees from high to low whereas the *inverse* is true of artists. They invert the proper ordering of their souls so that their sensual desires overwhelm their reason (605b). In that they have banished reason to the lowest part of the soul, their inverse psychic ordering is given topographical expression in Socrates' claim that the poets distort reality insofar as they see from low to high. So transformed into a rhetoric of linearity, artists thus see the kingdom of truth from what I have called an infernal view of divinity. And it is from this infernal view, that they commit the crimes of impiety.

In arguing this case in book 2, Socrates accuses the poets of transgressing two fundamental "laws and patterns for religious speech and writing" promulgated in his city of words. The first law establishes that the divine must always be represented as the creator only of good, never of evil. The second law similarly condemns any poet who represents the divine as either false or dissimulating. In addition to these two laws, Socrates also argues that the poetic meter used to describe the divine must reflect the beauty of its subject. In sum, the divine must therefore be represented as the apotheosis of the true, the good, and the beautiful. For Socrates, the poets' distortion of the gods reflected in their transgression of these laws may well be a consequence of their infernal inversion of reality. From the perspective of Socrates' inverted world, the poets thus stand condemned.

What may be held in honor in the Piraeus or even in Athens is certainly banished from Socrates' city of words. Indeed, their heads anointed with oil and their bodies wreathed with wool, the poets are led beyond the figurative walls of his *callipolis*. "We'll stick to our own austere and cheerless storyteller," Socrates tells us, "because he's beneficial: he imitates the speech of a decent man and frames his stories on those patterns we prescribed in the beginning" (398a-b). No doubt, shaped in accordance with the divine, these patterns are reflected in Plato's representation of Socrates' city as a drama of the good and noble life.

Plato's Ironic Art

It would be difficult to believe that Plato did not recognize the irony implicit in his own artistry. In constructing Socrates' drama of the good and noble life in the *Republic*, for example, he consciously appears to compare himself to those "painters who paint in accord with the divine model." Such artists will begin by taking "a city and human dispositions as if they were a tablet and first wipe it clean. . . . Next they sketch an outline of the regime and then fill it in, constantly looking back and forth to that which by nature is the just, the beautiful, the temperate, and so on" (501a-c). In imitating the divine, Plato represents Socrates representing the forms. Displacing the poets, Plato thus places himself three removes from the divine realm of the *eidos*. Indeed, consciously adopting an ironic stance to his own art, Plato goes on to tell us that the forms themselves are beyond all visual representation. For this reason, he seems to suggest, an art seeking to represent the forms can never adequately express their presence.[9] The paradox is apparent. Plato's representation of Socrates' art must unveil, bring to presence, and make apparent the nonrepresentational realm of the forms.

In representing that which is beyond representation, Plato has Socrates employ a series of images that attempt to translate the *eidos* into linguistic signs that can be grasped by human perception. Here, of course, I have in mind his famous images of the sun, line, and cave. These images clearly represent the nonrepresentational through visual analogy. In a more general respect, Socrates' *callipolis* itself may be understood as an allegory, a dramatized metaphor attempting to depict in linguistic form the nonrepresentational experience of the soul's turning "away from the world of becoming" into the eternal realm of true being (518d).

From this perspective, as an allegory, the forms signify the recovery of the pure visibility of the realm of truth, undisguised by the images projected by traditional poetry. It is an attempt to present the thing itself—not particular instances of the good but the good itself directly acting in the moral world it also defines. As antitragic, it is a drama of the pure intellect, a drama that carries us to a realm of invulnerability where the opposition and differences in the actual world are transformed into illusions. Against the passions of the actual, Socrates thus seems to offer a cascade of light as a reflection of divine intellect. Dissolving the tensions and contradictions of the world, he depicts the triumph of the philosophical spirit in reconciling the forces at play in the social, natural, and supernatural worlds. Such reconciliation is given a determinate shape in the most powerful image of his "true tragedy"—the divine realm of the forms.

In shaping his antitragic drama of the good and noble life, however, Socrates is parasitic upon the very darkness and arbitrariness that underlies, and thus makes possible, his representation of the forms as the realm of light, order, and presence.[10] It is a copy of the perceived world, changed into its opposite. In this way, the eternal, universal, and immutable qualities of the forms find their initial source not in the infinite but in the finite, particular, and mutable elements of the actual world (the sensible or perceived world). The divine reflection he offers is thus in reality a reflection of the actual world transformed through Plato's poetics of inversion. Far from taking flight from the realities of the political and ethical life of Athens, then, Socrates perceives the darkness that ultimately fosters his vision of health.

In this respect, Plato's articulation of Socrates' vision of the forms may amount to little more than a noble lie. Even though the poets cannot depict the gods as lying, Socrates reminds us that it is frequently useful for rulers to tell noble lies as a remedy for the disease in the souls of the ruled. He defines a "true" lie as "ignorance in the soul of the deceived" and a noble lie as a linguistic imitation that "likens the false to the true" for the purpose of edification. Obviously, as an imitation of the divine, Socrates' art cannot present the true in itself. Indeed, it may not even *re*-present the "true" for if Socrates' inversion of the sensible is, in reality, a reaction to the actual, then his art can neither emanate from nor reflect the divine. Witnessing the pain at the heart of the world, his "linguistic likening of the divine" thus appears as an artistic and ethical reaction shaped by the suffering of that which exists.

To put this point in more formal terms, Socrates' city of words, as an allegory, is by definition a dramatized metaphor that brings likeness to unlike things. In these terms, his city of words itself reflects the structure of a noble lie as a likening of the divine. But even from a rather cursory examination of his image of the sun, we find that in Socrates' own articulation of the metaphorical structure of the forms, his art appears not as a mirror but as a veil.

Referring to the traditional problem of the one and the many, Socrates begins his analysis of the forms as metaphor by claiming that:

> We say beautiful things and good things and so forth are many, and so define them in our speech. Then we turn around and say there's a beautiful itself, a good itself, and so on for all the things we then classed as many—we posit a single idea for each class, assuming it to be a unity and call it "that which is." And we say the manys are visible but not intelligible; the forms intelligible but not visible. (507b-c)

Here we have revealed on a linguistic level the forms as likenesses drawn from unlike things: A class that exhibits visible differences (the many) is unified by an abstract, universal concept that establishes a linguistic link between its components. Hence, the forms as intelligible provide the terms of identity by virtue of which "the many" gain their significance.

However, as an abstract identity, the forms seem to efface the very differences upon which they are linguistically constructed. In this respect, Socrates' vision of the forms may be seen to constitute a narrative grammar that hides the opposition and differences upon which the logic of his structure is, in fact, predicated. In terms of this structure, differences appear to lose their independent reality and significance insofar as they exist outside the figurative boundaries of Socrates' city of words. In other words, such differences become indeterminate and unbounded precisely because they are excluded from the boundary and determinacy of Socrates' city. In creating his linguistic field as the whole of the *logoi*, Socrates seems to offer human beings a vision of unity and stability that could persist only insofar as the indeterminacy of difference could be prevented from attaining significance.

By blotting out these differences, Socrates appears not only to banish tragic art from his own city of words but to banish tragedy itself. This idea is perhaps best exemplified in his recommendations regarding the community of guardians. Consider the conflict between kinship and citizenship that is often raised to the surface in classical tragedy. In Homer, for example, the beauty and pain of this conflict is expressed in the *Iliad* when, Hektor, returning from the battle, visits his wife and their son for perhaps the last time.

After Andromache pleads with her husband to remain at home, protected by the walls of Ilion, Hektor turns to look at his young son. Peering up at his father, who is still wearing the armor of battle, his helmet shielding his face, Astyanax is terrified by the very emblem of Hektor's honor. Gently laughing at his son's fear, however, Hektor soon reveals himself. Laying his helmet on the ground, he tosses Astyanax in his arms and kisses him. He then offers a blessing to the gods on behalf of his son. In the context of his own impending doom, he looks up to the heavens and makes this chilling prayer:

> Zeus, and you other immortals, grant that this boy, who is my son, may be, as I am, pre-eminent among the Trojans, great in strength, as am I, and rule strongly over Ilion; and some day let them say of him: "He is better by far than his father," as he comes in from the fighting; and let him kill his enemy and bring home the blooded spoils, and delight the heart of his mother. (475-481)

The haunting and deeply ironic tone of these words is not only marked by the strange juxtaposition between Andromache's obvious sorrow and her expected "delight" in "blooded spoils" brought home from war. It is also captured in Hektor's repeated desire that, as he goes off to his own death, his son will one day become "as I am" on the field of honor. Yet, with this prayer, Hektor leaves his wife and son to confront his fate, to stake his life both for his own honor and for his home, knowing that the delicate balance between these two ethical claims will soon to be destroyed.

The tensions and dissonances of ethical life found in Homer's story of Hektor are made much more explicit in the uncompromising works of the classical tragedians. The careful balance articulated by Homer appears to erupt into violence and shattered conflict in Aeschylus' *Agamemnon*. And, of course, in perhaps its most famous expression, Sophocles portrayed the opposing claims of family and city, of kinship ties and honor, in the characters of Antigone and Creon, respectively.

As a negative analogue to tragedy, Socrates' community of guardians exemplifies an antitragic desire to overcome such oppositions. In his *callipolis*, he transforms and conflates the semantic fields and ethical spheres commonly associated with the city and the family. Through the philosophical appropriation of these spheres, he constructs a vision of order and unity that always seems to end happily.

Happy Endings and Noble Lies

As we have seen in the case of Achilleus, Socrates transforms conventional attitudes of honor by questioning the traditional heroic ethos of the warrior. Guardians must learn to retard their delight in the bloody spoils of war. They must learn to stake their honor not on appearance but on their integrity to higher principles. Through the refinement of the intellect, Socrates claims, their uncontrolled desire and passion for blood could be constrained. Hence, with the proper education of their souls, Socrates seems to promise a transvaluation of the predominantly male ethos of the warrior.

Of course, it is not only the conventional values associated with men that Socrates places into question. Even more vehemently, he attacks the traditional attributes associated with women. Regardless of gender, the guardians of his city must never, he tells us, imitate a woman in any way whatsoever: "whether old or young, whether railing against her husband or boasting of a happiness which she imagines can rival the gods', or overwhelmed with grief and misfortune; much less a woman in love, or sick, or in labor" (395d-e). It therefore follows that, like their male counterparts, women must learn to resist imitating those characteristics conventionally associated with women.[11]

If, however, they fail in this lesson and imitate those values traditionally held by women, the harmonic structure of Socrates' community as a whole would be threatened. Through such imitation, they would invert the proper order of rule and allow their bodies and emotions to "install an evil regime" in their souls by gratifying the "irrational" (605c-e). Like the tyrant Socrates describes as "living the life of a woman," such women would destroy the state (579b-c).

In opposing the imitation of attributes he assigns to both men and women, he insists that the guardians should act only their own part and imitate only those qualities befitting their character:

> If we want to keep to our original idea, that our guardians must be freed from all other crafts to be expert craftsmen of the city's freedom, pursuing nothing that doesn't contribute to this end, then they must not do or imitate anything else. If they imitate anything, they must from childhood on imitate only what is appropriate to their function as guardians: courage, temperance, freedom, piety, and so on. They must shun the clever imitation of slavish or shameful acts as they would the acts themselves, to avoid reaping reality from imitation. (395c-d)

In this passage, the "original idea" to which Socrates refers is, of course, the principle of specialization.

Recall that Socrates' principle is based not on convention (*nomos*) but on the fundamental connection between nature (*physis*) and excellence (*aretē*): Individuals' excellence or potential for *aretē* is defined in terms of their *physis*, their natural capacities. Their natural capacity, in turn, is defined by that which they do as well or better than others. On the basis of these definitions, Socrates thus claims that individuals ought to perform that function and activity of excellence for which they are most suited. By appealing to nature as the determining characteristic of a person, Socrates could thus reject as purely conventional the attributes commonly associated with the sexes.

In book 5 of the *Republic*, however, the principle of specialization itself is raised as a possible criticism in what Socrates calls the "first wave of laughter" that is bound to come from his proposal that both women and men be adopted into the community of guardians. In terms of his proposal to include women in his community, Socrates appears quite serious when he entertains the criticism that on the basis of the principle of specialization, women can be excluded from a common system of education. For instance, responding to the claims made against his "ridiculous" notion that women should be seen naked next to men in exercise, Socrates replies:

> It is better to strip than to veil all things that cause laughter [*gel-*] in the eyes of the foolish. When reason reveals what is best, such laughter [*gel-*] fades away. This makes it plain that only a fool speaks of anything laughable [*gel-*] other than that which is evil. Such a fool tries to raise a laugh [*gel-*] by looking to an absurd pattern of folly and wrong rather than seriously following a standard of the beautiful as the mark of the good. (452d-e)

On the larger issue regarding the so-called natural differences of the sexes, he goes on to claim that not every manifest difference between persons is relevant to their respective capacities to do well and fare well in their tasks. In his view, the apparent differences between the sexes are not relevant in terms of their natural capacities.

Indeed, in regard to their nature (*physis*), he concludes, women do not qualitatively differ from men (453b-c).

Socrates may well be correct in arguing that biological differences should not be considered relevant to the excellence of performance in the tasks and projects of human beings. But the central problem of his scheme is located in his use of the principle of specialization to make this argument. As Aristotle pointed out, by defining one's excellence (*aretē*) in terms of one's nature (*physis*), Socrates condenses and reduces the complex functions performed in ethical life into a single integrative vision of political community, a whole bound together by suspiciously simple principles of unity. Of course, there is more than an obvious loss of functional complexity in this model. Aristotle's point is that in constructing his vision, Socrates fundamentally eliminates the significance of values appropriate to different spheres of human activity and conduct.

We should not be too quick, however, to endorse Aristotle's own position. After all, his stress on social differentiation is used to support a hierarchy of power based on gender differentiation. On this score, Socrates' position might appear more justifiable: At least in his hierarchical scheme women can be on top. Of course, looking back on it, both Socrates and Aristotle certainly can be faulted for advocating systems of structural inequality. In addition, Aristotle can be further criticized for supporting the proposition that "a woman's place is in the *oikos*." Nevertheless, his criticism that Socrates' city is based on the elimination of values associated with different spheres of activity is instructive.

Consider, for instance, how Socrates responds to the "second wave of ridicule." Instead of arguing that both male and female guardians should respect the values traditionally associated with kinship ties, Socrates claims that these attachments should be completely eliminated. Indeed, in his eugenic model the blood ties of the guardians are to be effaced. In what appears to be an attempt to avoid the experience of the inner division created by the challenge of the values of the family to the harmony of the political community, Socrates devises a scheme that would conceal the bonds between parents and children. In the community thus established, each would consider all the rest as bound to the *polis* as a whole. In this respect, his *callipolis* itself would allegedly become one big happy family.

In this harmonic structure, we are once again presented with Socrates' vision of "true tragedy," a drama of the good and noble life that conflates the differences between the values we attach to the *oikos* and those we associate with the polis. Yet precisely by depicting Socrates as wiping out such differences, Plato ironically seems to call attention to them. By ascending to the realm of the forms, he has the philosopher shed light on the contradictions, polarities, and divisions that are conspicuously absent from his own ideal narrative. Providing a happy ending to Socrates' true tragedy, he thus calls into question the very conflicts Socrates appears to resolve. At the same time, he also seems to question the verity of Socrates' own ideal vision.

Plato's use of animal imagery and jokes often serve this latter purpose.[12] For example, in his eugenic model, Socrates is persistently made to use metaphors of breeding and animal husbandry. "In a happy state, disorder and promiscuity in these unions is an unhallowed thing," Socrates tells us, "and the rulers will not suffer it" (458e). In demonstrating that the "sacred marriages" arranged by the rulers are most beneficial to the community, he likens the union of the guardians to the breeding of hunting dogs and pedigree cocks. If the best are not bred with the best in their prime, Socrates warns, what is worthy in the breed of birds, dogs, horses, and all other animals will greatly degenerate. By so obviously juxtaposing the sacred nature of marriage with the breeding of tame animals, Plato seems to calls attention to the dehumanization implicit in Socrates' proposal. Lost in such proposals are the fragile bonds of love and tenderness that Homer depicted between Andromache, Hektor, and their son. While stripping the bodies of his guardians, Socrates no doubt veils these bonds. His veil, however, is so thin and conspicuous that any Athenian would surely find his proposals laughable.

In addition to Plato's use of animal imagery, he also employs jokes to problematize Socrates' ideal. Exemplifying his desire to eviscerate the distinction between what is "one's own" and "not one's own" in his community, Socrates claims that his guardians should be so sensitized to the whole that if one member cuts his finger, the entire community would, in unison, yell, "Ouch!" Of course, such a scene belongs on the comic stage. Obviously, it is precisely because of the impossibility of overcoming the very real barriers of one's own bodily sensitivity to one's own pain that Socrates' endorsement of his own scheme is called into question. To seriously think of one's own in terms of an abstract relation to the city and its other members, no doubt eliminates a traditional source of value conflict. But, Plato ironically suggests, it also eliminates the irreducible and irreplaceable value we feel toward our own flesh and blood, toward our particular family members, friends, and city. In this way, Plato exposes the very sources of conflict that Socrates' ideal too obviously conceals.

The Limits of Irony in Plato's *Republic*

Plato's use of irony reaches its fullest exposure in his declaration that true tragedy always ends happily. Indeed, his recollection of Socrates' death ironically appears to offer just such a happy ending. Through his death, Socrates is said to have married divine love. Indeed, from Diotima he learns that *thanatos* and *eros* are not hostile and opposed forces but are ultimately joined together in the realm of the immortal. Recall the final words of Diotima's dissertation: "And since we have agreed that the lover longs for the good to be his own forever, it follows that we are bound to long for immortality as well as for the good—which is to say that Love is a longing for immortality" (*Symposium* 207a). In the fusion of love and death, in the rebirth of his own spirit, Plato recounts, Socrates had found that for which he had been preparing all of his life: the ascent to the divine realm of the forms.

The spirit of irony in Plato's recollection is inscribed in his use of the term *pharmakon* to describe the hemlock Socrates was to consume in his final moments of life. As Derrida has pointed out, *pharmakon* can be translated as either "poison" or "remedy."[13] Underscoring the change with his final reference to Asclepius, the healer, at the end of the *Phaedo*, Socrates transforms the image of poison associated with death into a divine remedy predicated on the soul's immortality. Yet Plato ironically undermines this antitragic portrait; Socrates' vertical ascent (*anabasis*) to a realm of invulnerability appears devoid of those attachments to life that are recognizably human. In contrast to Socrates' search for a stable, pure, and true world, Plato reminds us that we inhabit a world bounded by our vulnerability, fragility, and finitude.

Moreover, on a political level, Socrates' city of words itself may be seen as a *pharmakon*. For Socrates, the Peloponnesian War was a violent teacher. Under conditions of *stasis*, he learned that civilization could hold within itself all the cruelty of the beast world. He witnessed what Thucydides described as the "extravagances of revolutionary zeal," expressed by both "extreme ingenuity in seizing power" and "monstrosities committed in gaining revenge." With the change of events, Thucydides tells us, words, too, changed their meaning. "What used to be described as a thoughtless act of aggression came to be regarded [as] courage"; "circumspection and patience meant that one was a coward"; and "any idea of moderation was just an attempt to disguise one's unmanly weakness."[14] Accompanying human savagery and this loss of meaning was the specter of internal conflict that divided cities and left them ruined. Witnessing these events, Socrates offers us an antidote to the brutality, incoherence, and chaos of the past.

As an antitragic artist, he envisions a city shaped in accord with the divine patterns of intellectual verity, linguistic purity, and political harmony. Employing the language of the divine, however, Socrates reduces the complexity of human meaning into simple univocality. He overcomes the conflicts of political life, but he does so only by conflating the realms of our activity into an hierarchical structure based on the principle of specialization. Hence, in administering his cure, in saving us from the beast world by lifting us to the divine, Socrates' remedy drains the human world of its distinctive qualities and fragile attachments.

Lost is the richness, complexity, and indeterminacy of our position as human beings *entre bêtes et dieux*. Recognizing this loss, Plato himself places Socrates' cure into question. If true tragedy invariably ends happily, he reminds us, such happy endings themselves are often less than noble lies. Just as Alcibides' "comic" discourse on love compromises Socrates' pure vision in the *Symposium*, Plato problematizes Socrates' serious proposals in the *Republic*. In this respect, happy endings are never reassuring. Indeed, compromise, resignation, doubt, frank disbelief, and denial seem to be indispensable ingredients in Plato's art. Like the tragedians Socrates banishes, Plato questions Socrates' ideals by illuminating the vulnerability, linguistic opacity, and ethical conflict that remain veiled in his city of words. Through comedy, he also calls into question Socrates' desire for "happiness" and the "forever after": "He who knows how to produce tragedy by art would also know how to produce comedy." In depicting Socrates' antitragic theater, Plato no doubt qualifies as just such an artist.

Ironically employing comic and tragic themes, Plato frustrates and forestalls the philosophical closure that linguistically bounds Socrates' city. Yet there is a final paradox inherent in Plato's use of irony. Parasitic on that which it deconstructs, the more Plato disrupts the linguistic boundaries of Socrates' city, the closer he draws us back to the familiar ground of Socrates' vision. By constructing that which he deconstructs, Plato ironically confirms that which he denies. Indeed, with the simultaneous yes and no of the ironic mode, with its repetition of that which it subverts, Plato's art can never escape the language of Socrates' *callipolis*. Trapped in this unending dynamic, he continually resurrects Socrates' antitragic vision only to once again undermine it in an endless play of irony. In this respect, Plato both tells and untells the antitragic tale told by Socrates. But, he does not provide us with a way of escaping the "undecidability" of Socrates' city. At the horizons of Socrates' *callipolis*, which wavers back and forth between cure and poison, we reach the limits of irony in Plato's *Republic*.[15]

Notes

1. Citations to Plato's works are from the *Loeb Classical Library*, ed. T. E. Page (Cambridge, Mass.: Harvard University Press, 1914). Unless otherwise specified, translations are my own.

2. Rather than focusing on the "Socratic question," I will represent Socrates as a character who, at least in the *Republic*, is most closely associated with antitragic art; i.e., what the Athenian Stranger calls "true tragedy." Whatever its defects, this approach has the advantage of being "literally" accurate. Whether or not Plato's is an accurate portrait of the historical Socrates, in his dialogues, Socrates is without question a character with distinct diction and thought. I discuss the full significance of the structure of representation—Plato representing Socrates representing true tragedy—in Part 3 below.

3. *The Iliad*, trans. Richmond Lattimore (Chicago: University of Chicago Press, 1951), Bk. 9, lines 405-416. I have used Richard Lattimore's translation of the *Iliad* throughout this chapter.

4. Here I am following Hugh Tredennick's rendering of *thanatôsi* as "half-dead." See his translation of the *Phaedo* in *The Collected Dialogues of Plato*, ed. Edith Hamilton and Huntington Cairns (Princeton: Princeton University Press, 1961).

5. For a full definition of the relationship between irony and allegory as used in this context, see Paul de Man, "The Rhetoric of Temporality," in *Interpretation: Theory and Practice*, ed. Charles S. Singleton (Baltimore: Johns Hopkins University Press, 1969), 173-209.

6. For example, see Eric Voegelin, *Plato* (Baton Rouge: Louisiana State University Press, 1960), 59.

7. Simon Goldhill, *Reading Greek Tragedy* (Cambridge: Cambridge University Press, 1986), 74.

8. As Plato depicts it, Socrates' educational scheme is based on his ability to impress the virtues appropriate to the nature of the souls being educated. Here we find Socrates' reliance on the principle of specialization applied to moral education. For a critical assessment of the principle of specialization, see part 4 below.

9. John Freccero has captured the paradox implicit in such artistry: "Every imitation of the real carries with it the potentiality of irony," he tells us, "because representation can never be presentation; its very existence denies its identity with its object." See his *Dante, the Poetics of Conversion* (Cambridge, Mass.: Harvard University Press, 1986), 108.

10. Here I am following the basic deconstructive strategy established by Paul de Man in his essay on "Pascal's Allegory of Persuasion," in *Allegory and Representation*, ed. Stephen Greenblatt (Baltimore: Johns Hopkins University Press, 1981), 1-26.

11. For a similar view, see Froma Zeitlin's article, "Playing the 'Other,'" in *Representations* 11 (Summer 1985): 63-94.

12. For a more detailed account, see Arlene Saxonhouse, "Comedy in *Callipolis*: Animal Imagery in the *Republic*," *American Political Science Review* 72 (September 1978): 888-901.

13. See Derrida's discussion in "La pharmacie de Platon," *Tel Quel* 32 (Winter 1968), 3-49.

14. Thucydides, *Peloponnesian War* (Cambridge, Mass.: Loeb Classical Library, 1912), bk. 3, ch. 82, lines 3-4.

15. The implications of the limits of irony I have ascribed to Plato's *Republic* are more fully discussed in "A Carnival of Critics" (Chapter 5) and "Putting the "E" Back into *Différance*" (Chapter 7).

2

Rousseau and the Echoes of *Narcisse*

It is not surprising that Jean-Jacques Rousseau, a self-proclaimed *"homme à paradox"* and a notorious critic of the theatrical arts, began his career as a playwright.[1] His first work was entitled, *Narcisse*. Written at Chambéry when Rousseau was in his early twenties, this play was not produced until after his opera *Le Devin du village* was successfully performed before the king at Fontainebleau in 1753. Unattributed to an author, *Narcisse* closed without distinction after its second performance at the *Comédie Française*. During intermission at the play's opening, we are told, Rousseau left the theater shouting that the author of such a work must have been a raving fool (*devin*).[2]

Inspired by Voltaire's *Indiscret* (1725) and perhaps Marivaux's *Petit Maître corrige* (1736), *Narcisse* is a stylish comedy of manners. It is the story of a young man, Valère, who on his wedding day falls in love with a portrait of himself dressed as a woman. The portrait was placed in Valère's chamber by his sister, Lucinde, who wants to teach him a lesson about his excessive vanity. However, rather than learning this lesson, Valère, unaware that the portrait is a reflection of himself, declares that he will not be married until he finds the woman portrayed. He searches throughout Paris for this remarkable woman, obviously in vain. Finally his fiancée, Angélique, forces Valère to choose between her and the subject of the portrait. He eventually chooses Angélique, who then explains to him that he was enamored with his own reflection. Valère having acknowledged the problem of his vanity, the couple are married and Valère vows that in the future he will "love the subject of the portrait only insofar as that subject loves another." In this way, Rousseau tell us, although it is better to love nothing than to be in love with oneself ("*il vaux mieux n'aimer rien que d'être amoureux de soi-même*"), it is better still to love oneself only insofar as one loves another (ii 1002). With the recognition of this lesson, *Narcisse* appears to end happily.

However, through ridiculing the character of Valère, the reconciliation scene of *Narcisse* conceals the tension inherent in the paradoxical relationship Rousseau establishes between Valère's self-love and his self-estrangement. In general, the mirroring effect of narcissistic self-reflection may well call to mind the tautology of perfect self-reference: the Fichtean "I=I". As a form of self-presence, it implies an immediate recognition of the self in its image. And yet narcissism in Rousseau (as in Ovid) is never an immediate experience of the self's presence. For in the experience of self-love, Rousseau believed, there is always a gap between the representer and the represented, the spectator and the spectacle or, in more contemporary terms, between the signifier and the signified. This gap allows for the disruption of self-reference. It provides the area of mediation that transforms the image into an accurate representation of the self's distortion. Hence in *Narcisse*, the portrait of Valère is not subjectively distorted; rather, it is Valère's self-distortion that is objectively portrayed. In other words, the portrait as an (external) image of Valère's self-love is a reflection of Valère's (inner) self-distortion.

In Rousseau's view, such distortion is inherent in the experience of self-love. Indeed, he defined vanity or self-love as the desire to be identified as an object of admiration. In this respect, one's identity becomes inseparably bound to one's status as an object for others. But the identification of oneself as an object for others mediates and perverts simple self-reference. It forces one to rely on the recognition of others to affirm one's identity and establish one's self-esteem. Paradoxically, then, though he is obviously self-possessed, we find Valère constantly attempting to please others in order to gain their admiration, which, in turn, he uses only to bolster his own self-love and self-absorption.

Insofar as Valère draws the sentiments of his own existence from other's perceptions of him, he remains forever outside himself. In spatial terms, Valère's self-love is thus a form of self-estrangement. He is transported outside himself and remains a stranger to himself. Indeed, he is a prisoner of his own self-objectification. In temporal terms, Rousseau describes this same process as one of self-forgetfulness, the inability to recollect oneself that results from identifying oneself as an object of consciousness for others. In this way, Rousseau forges the bonds between self-love, on the one hand, and self-estrangement and self-forgetfulness, on the other.

In *Narcisse*, Valère's estrangement and forgetfulness is manifested through an inverted form of the natural order: the effeminization of his character. Indeed, Rousseau describes Valère explicitly "by his delicacy and affectation, a sort of woman," he tells us, "hidden under the clothes of a man" (ii 977). For Rousseau, Valère is a victim of self-dissimulation and mystification. He identifies himself with feminine characteristics that could not reflect his inner nature. And yet it is only through the women, Angélique and Lucinde, that Valère can overcome his self-estrangement. In this respect, the role of women in *Narcisse* seems to be that of creating the conditions under which Valère comes to recognize himself as a man. And with such awareness, he thereafter embraces the duties and conjugal bonds appropriate to his condition.

Rather than sexual self-absorption, Rousseau is no doubt arguing for a kind of sexual interdependence. But we should not be too hasty in celebrating Rousseau's commitment to such interdependence.[3] Although Valère's self-recognition is dependent on the lesson taught by women, women themselves have very little opportunity to shape their own actions in Rousseau's world. At best, they are the teachers of morals, but they are rarely moral actors. Because women arouse men's desires and establish the bonds of love, men become dependent upon women. In this way, women use the most "terrible and dangerous" of men's passions to gain authority over men's hearts (iii 157). But, Rousseau insisted, women ought to apply their sexual power didactically. That is to say, they ought to rule men only insofar as they use the "violence of their charms" to "constrain men to exhibit their strengths" (iv 693f.). Through this process, Rousseau believed, men dispel their self-illusions and learn to reflect the truth of themselves in their conduct. In short, they learn to reflect in the world the externalization of their inner will.

We thus find Lucinde and Angélique in *Narcisse* using the charms and modesty of their sex to force Valère to confront and finally to conquer the illusions of his self-image. In this respect, *Narcisse* is a didactic play. But its lessons are not confined to its sexual themes or narrative structure. Rather, as the preface to his play indicates, Rousseau intends to mirror the vanity of the Parisian audience he professes to entertain.[4] Moreover, the protagonist of *Narcisse* is linked to Rousseau's characterization of social estrangement, insofar as Valère imitates the estrangement inherent in the role of the dramatic actor who, in turn, reflects the vanity of his audience that collectively, in the end, mirrors the estrangement of social experience. Rousseau thus portrays the theater as itself a reflection of the vanity and estrangement of his age. Indeed, he characterizes his society as a kind of theater where all assume alien roles and project themselves as objects to be admired in the eyes of others. In his words: "It is . . . solely for these people that theatrical entertainments are made. They are represented by fictitious characters in the middle of the theater and show themselves in real ones on each side; they are at once persons of the drama on the stage and the comedians in the boxes."[5] Through this mirroring effect, Rousseau's phenomenology of the theater offers a dramaturgical critique of the social experience of self-estrangement.

Phenomenology of the Theater

In important respects, Rousseau was deeply influenced by his reading of Plato's criticism of the arts in the *Republic*.[6] Like Socrates, for instance, he argued against the theatrical imitation of those strong passions that excite the soul and "soil the imagination."

"The only instrument which can serve to purge them is reason," he tells us, and "reason has no effect in the theater" (*PA* 21). In addition to his advocacy of Socrates' antitragic approach to the display of passion, Rousseau explicitly links self-estrangement to the criticism of poetic *mimesis* depicted in the tenth book of the *Republic*. Recasting Socrates' use of the metaphor of distance into a description of estrangement, he thus claims: "The foundation of imitation among us comes from the desire always to transport ourselves outside ourselves" (iii 360). In Rousseau's view, the estrangement resulting from this process characterizes the phenomenology of the dramatic actor. "What is the talent of the actor?" he asks in his *Lettre à M. d'Alembert*:

> It is the art of counterfeiting himself [he replied], of putting on a character other than his own, of appearing different than he is, of becoming passionate in cold blood, of saying what he does not think as naturally as if he really did think it, and finally, of forgetting his own place by dint of taking another's.[7]

As Plato depicts Socrates' attack in the *Ion*, Rousseau argues that orienting oneself toward the exterior features of another, imitating a character's external gestures and appearance, implies turning away from oneself, away from what one is inwardly. Such imitation is thus accomplished through self-forgetfulness. But, insofar as the actor is fully immersed in his or her role, imitation does not simply consist in representing the exteriority of the character portrayed. Rather, the actor's art is carried out as self-dissimulation. In this respect, the actor experiences the imitation of an "alien" exterior as the annihilation and loss of self. In other words, the actor does not merely act out someone else's gestures. On the contrary, all the actor's expressions are the display of an inner will that is nevertheless not the actor's own will. According to this phenomenology of self-forgetfulness, imitation therefore fulfills itself as self-estrangement.[8] As Rousseau puts it: "An actor on the stage, displaying other sentiments than his own, saying only what he is made to say, often representing an illusory being, annihilates himself, as it were, and is lost in his hero" (*PA* 81).

Just as the actor experiences a form of self-estrangement through his or her dissimulation, Rousseau claims, the spectators also lose themselves in the performance. That is, even those who merely watch such imitation without acting themselves yield to the spectacle in sympathy, which is to say, they forget themselves in vicariously experiencing the Other whom they see before them. Hence, in contrast to Aristotle's focus on pity as that in virtue of which members of the audience vicariously engage in the suffering of others "like them," Rousseau argues that such sympathy for another's suffering ultimately results in the complete self-disengagement of the audience, the loss of self in experiencing the Other.

And yet, like Aristotle, Rousseau often commends what he calls "*l'impulsion intérieure de la commisération*" (the interior impuse of commiseration) that transports us outside ourselves and allows us to identify with a being who suffers (iii 126). But, as Aristotle knew, to feel such commiseration, we must not only be transported by the suffering of the Other, we must also experience the Other's anxiety for ourselves. That is to say, pity is possible only by recognizing what the self has in common with the Other. For Rousseau, however, it is precisely this engagement that is missing from the theatrical experience of *pitié*. Indeed, because it lacks such recollection of the self in the suffering of the Other, Rousseau proclaims, the audience's sympathy is only a "fleeting and vain emotion which lasts no longer than the illusion which produced it" (*PA* 25). In this way, tracing what he saw as Plato's ontological description of theatrical imitation as illusion, Rousseau claims that the audience loses itself in the character without the fear of experiencing the shared basis of the suffering portrayed. Although the theater may carry our emotions to sublime heights, it will never allow us to feel real sympathy. In Rousseau's words:

> If . . . the heart is more readily touched by feigned ills than real ones, if theatrical imitations draw forth more tears than would the presence of the objects imitated, it is less because the emotions

are feebler and do not reach the level of pain . . . than because they are pure and without mixture of anxiety for ourselves. In giving our tears to these fictions, we have satisfied all the rights of humanity without having to give anything more of ourselves; whereas unfortunate people in person would require attention for us, relief, consolation, and work, which would involve us in their pains and would require at least the sacrifice of our indolence, from all of which we are quite content to be exempt. It could be said that our heart closes itself for fear of being touched at our expense. (*PA* 25)

For Rousseau, the intense emotions felt in the theater paradoxically distance us from the concerns of our common humanity. In this respect, he believes that by provoking our passions "everything that is played in the theater is not brought nearer to us, but made more distant" (*PA* 25). Indeed, in his view, the theater isolates us from our fellow human beings: "People think they come together in the theater, and it is there that they are isolated. It is there that they go to forget their friends, neighbors, and relations in order to concern themselves with fables, in order to cry for the misfortunes of the dead, or to laugh at the expense of the living" (*PA* 16).

In the end, Rousseau argues that both the actor and the spectator experience the theater as self-estrangement. Both are captured in a hall of mirrors that nonetheless cannot reflect their inner wills. And both experience the illusory joys of self-forgetfulness that reflect their estrangement. Under such conditions, the mirror is the most confining of cells. When we look into one, we see ourselves bounded by our own image. There we are alone while remaining estranged from ourselves. Multiply the mirrors, as the theater does, and you create a monstrosity, a world in which the man who is running toward his own self-reflection is always running away from himself. Such a man is like Valère, an emblematic figure of the theatrical art of social experience.[9]

The Politics of Love and Estrangement

In the *Discours sur l'origine de l'inégalité*, Rousseau reconstructs the past in accordance to the lost ideals of "natural" pity and "natural" love of oneself (*amour de soi*). In this respect, he attempts to recollect what is lost in the self-forgetfulness of estrangement. Indeed, reflecting the spirit of Augustine's *Confessions*, Rousseau's *Discours* is based on the paradox of recovering what one does not and cannot remember losing.[10] But whereas Augustine's personal odyssey is a rediscovery of that which he did not realize he had lost until he found it, the structure of Rousseau's analysis is further complicated in that the vision of nature recollected in the *Discours* "never actually existed" even in a prelapsarian past. In this respect, his depiction of the state of nature is not at all a "naive" vision of the self's unmediated representation.[11] It is, rather, a fiction self-consciously constructed as a negative image of human corruption. In other words, Rousseau does not diagnose the ills of human society from the perspective of an unmediated condition of nature; instead, he gives his diagnosis of human corruption a fictionalized analogue in his conception of nature. In this respect, as we shall see, pity for Rousseau is the "natural" analogue of amorous passion and love of oneself (*amour de soi*) is the salubrious counterpart to the social disease of human vanity.

The pity lost in the experience of the theater is reclaimed in Rousseau's state of nature. There, pity is seen as the "sole natural virtue" (iii 154). Because it precedes all human reflection, it does not attach itself to an object based on comparison, preference, differentiation or particularity. Indeed, pity is a generalized sentiment that derives from our own love of self and embraces those like us. For this reason, he argues, the virtue of "*l'humanité*" itself is nothing other than "pity applied to the human species in general," which "even the most depraved morals we see daily in our theaters still have difficulty destroying" (iii 155).

Yet there is one element that possesses the power to destroy natural pity. In Rousseau's view, pity is threatened neither by *thanatos* nor by a spirit of aggression, but by that "impetuous ardor . . . so often fatal for men"—love:

> Of the passions that agitate the heart of man, there is one, both ardent and impetuous, that makes the sexes necessary to each other; a terrible passion that braves danger, overcomes all obstacles, and in its transports seems calculated to destroy the human species which it is really destined to preserve. What must become of men who are left to this brutal and boundless rage? (iii 157)

According to Rousseau, amorous passion is the perversion of natural pity. Unlike the latter, love is "fixed exclusively on a single object" of desire (iii 157f.). As we limit our attachment to this "preferred object," the evil that Rousseau associates with love takes on the familiar form of determination, comparison, and preference—that is to say, difference. As he puts it:

> People become accustomed to consider different objects and to make comparisons; imperceptibly they acquire ideas . . . which produce sentiments of preference. . . . A tender and gentle sentiment steals itself into the soul and is by the least opposition embroiled in impetuous fury. Jealousy awakens with love; discord triumphs, and the gentlest of the passions receives the sacrifices of human blood. (iii 169)

In Rousseau's view, women have the capacity to exploit men's love. Through their natural modesty, they have a greater capacity to control their passions than do men (iv 694). By resisting the affections of men, they self-consciously create obstacles for men to overcome. But by overcoming the resistances created by women, men become increasingly dependent upon women: "Love is the realm of women. It is they who necessarily give the law in it because according to the order of nature resistance belongs to them, and men can conquer this resistance only at the expense of their liberty" (*PA* 46).

As Derrida has suggested, love acts as a "strategem of femininity, an arresting of nature by woman."[12] An artificial sentiment born in society, love is thus at the service of women to establish their rule and secure men's obedience. In Rousseau's words: "Love is a factitious sentiment; born of social usage, and celebrated with much skill and care by women in order to establish their empire and render dominant the sex that ought to obey" (iii 158).

In the *Émile*, Rousseau tells us that nature made "women to please and to be subjugated by men" (iv 693). As in Hegel's master-slave dialectic, however, he claims that love reverses the polarities of sexual power. Through the ruses of love, he declares, "the stronger only appears to be master, while he actually depends upon the weaker" (iv 695f.).

Rousseau often associates women's power in modern society with that of the theater. He believes that both are involved in creating illusions, casting spells, and "charming" men. Given this association,

> a natural effect of [the theater] is to extend the empire of the fair sex, to make women and girls the preceptor of the public, and to give them the same power over the audience that they have over their lovers. Do you think, Sir, that this order is without its difficulties; and that, in taking so much effort to increase the ascendancy of women, men will be the better governed for it? (*PA* 46)

Rather than governing men well, Rousseau declares, women tend to make men effeminate. In this respect, he attributes men's effeminacy to the reversed valence of sexual power predominant in modern society.

In his *Discours*, Rousseau not only traces the corruption produced by the transitive experience of love, he also records the corruption of love in its self-reflexive form. For just as he envisions pity as a fictionalized analogue of amorous passion, Rousseau depicts the "natural" love of oneself as the uncorrupted analogue of human vanity. It should come as no surprise, then, that he associates the development of vanity with the "primitive" origins of theatricality. As social interaction became more frequent, he tells us:

> People grew accustomed to assembling in front of the huts or around a large tree; song and dance . . . became the amusement or rather the occupation of the idle gatherings of men and women. Each one began to notice the others and wanted to be noticed himself, and public esteem had a value. The one who sang or danced the best, the most handsome, the strongest, the most adroit, or the most eloquent became the most highly considered; and that was the first step toward inequality, and, at the same time, vice. From these first preferences were born . . . vanity and envy; and the fermentation caused by these new leavens at length produced compounds fatal to happiness and innocence. (iii 169f.)

Vanity, like passionate love, Rousseau argues, appears only with the development of society. "It is a relative, fictitious feeling which, arising only in society, leads the individual to make more of himself than any other and causes all the evil that men inflict on one another" (iii 219). In the *Discours*, Rousseau distinguishes vanity, or *amour propre*, from *amour de soi*, or the love of oneself. According to his analysis, *amour de soi* is an attribute of the self-conception of a person as a presocial being in the state of nature. Because such a "natural man," Rousseau writes, "considers himself as the sole Spectator of himself, the only being in the universe who takes an interest in him as the sole judge of his own merit, no sentiment which takes its source from comparisons . . . could take root in his soul" (iii 219).

Instead of displaying the natural disposition of *amour de soi*, this "social man" is not the sole judge of himself but is "always outside of himself, knows how to live only in the opinions of others; and it is, so to speak, from their judgment alone that he draws the sentiment of his own existence" (iii 193). The identity of the individual in society hence lies at the mercy of others: How they judge him determines how he judges himself. His status is therefore relative, and his self-love—*amour propre*—is dependent on his relative status (iii 222).[13] In this way, Rousseau's analysis of *amour propre* is linked to the process of self-objectification. As a condition of *amour propre*, self-recognition in society is based on the individual's status as an object of consciousness for others.

Confined within this prison-house of consciousness, human beings are transported outside of themselves and become strangers to themselves. Vanity (*amour propre*) thus reflects their self-estrangement. Ultimately, Rousseau argues, the distinctive capacity for estrangement is predicated on the spirit of human freedom and the faculty of perfectibility. Indeed, what distinguishes human beings from all other living species is their power to estrange themselves from their nature. Unlike other animals, which are simply impelled by the forces of nature, human beings can break the self-enclosed horizons of their natural independence and destroy the instinctual impulses of *amour de soi*. In this regard, human freedom appears as an act of the will capable of resisting and, indeed, perverting the instincts of nature. Pitted against the will, these instinctual forces constitute an ever-present obstacle and limitation to human perfectibility, the faculty by virtue of which humanity strives to overcome itself. The transgression of such limitations through an act of the will reveals what Rousseau calls the "spirituality of the human soul":

> Nature commands every animal, and the Beast obeys. Man is made to feel the same impulse, but he realizes that he is free to acquiesce or resist; and it is above all in the consciousness of this freedom that the spirituality of his soul reveals itself . . . [for] the power of willing, or rather of choosing is a purely spiritual act. (iii 141f.)

The spiritual act of human freedom is thus an expression of humanity's "infinitude," the unbounded power of the human will.[14] Yet there is little that distinguishes this "power to will" from the "will to power," as the spirituality of the soul entails the power to transgress any limitation that presents an obstacle or end to human power.[15]

Freedom, as the human will to change, transforms into open structures the determinate and self-enclosed actions that characterize humanity in its prereflective state. In this way, the horizons of perception are infinitely expanded through the development of the imagination. No longer bounded by the necessity and the simple impulsions of nature, humanity is locked into a dialectic of unfulfillable passions and an endless quest for knowledge (iii 143). As an effect of this transformation into the indeterminate, indefinite, and infinite, humanity is deprived of a central identity. Indeed, the continual expansion of passion, knowledge, and imagination can find no end except through "death and its terrors" (iii 143).

For Rousseau, our consciousness of the self-creation of our actions throws us into the "realm of time." In the words of Georges Poulet:

> Man no longer lives in a sort of absolute, no longer is limited to pure sensation, no longer is identified with nature, no longer confirms himself in the sole feelings of his actual existence. In addition to the present, the future and the past take form and invite comparisons and preferences. This is the kingdom of the relative, the kingdom of time.[16]

Once subjects in the kingdom of time, humans confronts the future with the dread of death and can look back to the past for the memory of the lost immediacy of the "natural man" who lives "in a state where time means nothing to it, where the present lasts forever" (*Julie* 232). In sum, human perfectibility and the spirituality of the soul revealed in the consciousness of freedom thus lead not to moral progress but to the dread of the future, the desire for unfulfillable passions, and the perversion and transgression of our own instinctual forces.

This notion of freedom, with its Faustian dimension of the self-appropriation of the world through the will, obviously presents vast difficulties for Rousseau's political community. In order to create the boundaries to this limitless freedom, human beings must themselves construct the horizons of their actions. In this way, the moral freedom of the community always implies at once both self-enslavement and liberation. In Rousseau's view, the only way to legitimately constrain the expansion of the centripetal forces of the human will is through an act of the will consecrated in the name of self-mastery. In the *Contrat social*, Rousseau thus declares that it is "moral freedom that alone truly renders man master of himself, for to be impelled only by appetite is slavery, while obedience to a law one prescribes to oneself is freedom" (iii 365). After giving this definition, he argues that as a citizen, each individual must directly participate in determining the laws, but as a subject of the state, each individual must obey the laws so determined. Hence, as subjects of the state, we obey the laws that, as citizens, we prescribe to ourselves.

From Rousseau's perspective, the constraint of the human will necessary for the realization of moral freedom requires nothing less than a "conversion experience." Rather than allowing one to identify with one's own independent status as a being capable of self-definition, moral freedom requires that each individual "alienate himself and his *powers* to the community as a whole" (iii 360). Unlike the self-totalizing existence of human independence found in the state of nature, in the "existential community" of the state, each citizen must derive his being and identity from his relation to the social whole. Employing metaphorically the language of mathematics, Rousseau thus claims: "Natural man is entirely for himself. He is the numerical unity, the absolute whole in its self-relation. . . . [The citizen, however] is only a fractional unity dependent upon the denominator and his value is related only to the whole—the body politic" (iv 249).

Rousseau's understanding of the citizen was obviously inspired by the ancients: "A citizen of Rome," he declares, "was neither Caius nor Lucius, but a Roman" (iv 249). Accepting the basic features of Aristotelian politics, Rousseau appears to reject Aristotle's concept of human nature only to reconstruct it on an artificial basis. For Rousseau, the individual must be "denatured," must relinquish his soul to the body politic. Only then does he exist as a citizen. And only from citizens, Rousseau believes, could the sacred name of the public good be guided. Alone the citizen is nothing. He derives his force and strength from his membership in a common life. In sum, he must sacrifice his nature to the laws of the state and renounce his natural sentiments to the sacred right of the body politic. Thus, unlike the natural man, whose self-conception is not affected either by his relations to others or by others' opinions of him, the citizen identifies himself as an integral part of the community: Who he is is determined by the character of the state of which he is a part.

Although Rousseau is undoubtedly aware of the loss of natural independence necessary to transform the individual into the citizen, he nonetheless believes that the valorization of the ontological status of the citizen would prevent the effects of *amour propre* from destroying the state. Indeed, by submerging the individual's identity with the community as a whole, Rousseau believes that he can devalue the particularity and difference that moves individuals to compare themselves with each other. This devaluation could not prevent *amour propre* from arising in the state, but it would attenuate the conflicts inspired by particularity, difference, and private interest. A citizen's personal ambitions would be directed toward the greater priority of the general good. Thus, one person would not experience another's achievement as a personal defeat: There would be no zero-sum game of social merit. Rather, all achievements would be hailed as tributes to the glory of the state as a whole.

The Politics of Narcissism

In Rousseau's view, the existence of freedom as self-mastery, with its attending conception of human identity based on the community, would resolve the problem of self-estrangement he associates with the modern age. But his vision of the civic community could dispel this problem only by constructing a "politics of narcissism." In Rousseau's civic community, each citizen, by determining the law, experiences the externalization of his inner will as a reflection of himself in the world. No doubt under such conditions, as Rousseau says, "the first man to propose a law is only articulating what everyone already feels" (iii 437), for in his state, one sees oneself only in the will of the community. Indeed, Rousseau defines *la volonté générale* as the will of the community as a whole as each citizen expresses it in determining the laws of the state. But in determining the general will, he argues, each citizen must think only his own thoughts. In this sense, laws are the objective expression of each citizen's inner will. By so expressing their will, citizens thus establish their determinate place and, to use a more modern phrase, are at home in Rousseau's world.

But, as Rousseau knows only too well, there is always a muscular tension of repression constantly threatening to disrupt his vision. The root of this tension is *amour propre* as it drives the human will toward particularity and difference. To relieve the body politic of this repressed energy, Rousseau advocates, among other institutions, the public festival. The festival serves to sustain the *moeurs* (ethical habits) and principles of the state by reaffirming *les sentiments de sociabilité* (the sentiments of sociability). As Mikhail Bakhtin explains, in contrast to the theater, the festival

> is by no means a purely artistic form nor a spectacle and does not, generally speaking, belong to the sphere of art. It belongs to the borderline between art and life. In reality, it is life itself, but shaped according to a certain pattern of play. . . . [It] is not a spectacle seen by the people; they live in it, and everyone participates because its very idea embraces all the people. . . . It has a universal spirit; it is a special condition of the entire world, of the world's revival and renewal, in which all take part.[17]

In a similar spirit, Rousseau claims that in public fêtes there exists no separation between spectator and spectacle that would lead to inner division and conflict. For this reason, he urges: "Let the spectators become an entertainment to themselves; make them actors themselves; do it so that each sees and loves himself in the others so that all will be better united" (*PA* 45).

As in taking political action, by directly participating in these festivals, the citizen "represents only himself, fills only his own role and speaks only in his own name" (*PA* 87). In the absence of self-dissimulation, Rousseau claims, such a citizen would not experience the loss of self inherent in the phenomenology of the theater. On the contrary, in a public fête, "everyone lives in the greatest familiarity; everyone is equal and no one forgets himself" (*Julie* 459). Thus, Rousseau argues, public festivals themselves become a ritualized form of collective self-recollection. Through their participation, citizens recall their commitments to social harmony. These rituals usually take the form of a marriage ceremony, a reconciliation and settlement of sexual differences that help to bolster the collective will of the state.

In protecting the purity of the collective will, women play their "proper role" as agents of moral *paideia*. Indeed, just as, in the *Emile*, Rousseau implores women to create a wall around the souls of their children, so in his political writings, he declares that women must protect citizens from relinquishing their virtue and identity. Paradoxically, he maintaines, they must channel men's erotic attachments away from the *oikos*, so that they may more firmly attach themselves to the *patria*, the "fatherland." Such erotic sublimation from feminine to masculine attachment is the lesson that Rousseau believes Spartan women taught their men. Indeed, it is the didactic principle of the following story as Rousseau relates it: "A Spartan woman had five sons in the army and was awaiting news of the battle. A Helot arrives, trembling, she asks him for news of the battle. 'Your five sons were killed,' he replied. 'Base slave, did I ask you that?' 'We won the victory.' The mother runs to the temple and gives thanks to the gods." This, Rousseau declares, "is the true female citizen!" (iv 249)

Through men's passionate dependence on women, women possess the power either to feminize or masculinize men. Under corrupt social conditions, Rousseau claims, "unable to make themselves into men, women make us into women" (*PA* 100f.). And yet as we have just seen in the example of the Spartan mother, women can also reenforce the masculine values of the state. In this way, women masculinize men in Rousseau's civic community (iv. 699f.). By constraining men to recognize and identify themselves with men and the state, Rousseau's "female citizens" echo the lessons Lucinde and

Angélique taught Valère in *Narcisse*. In this way, Rousseau appears to construct a form of social organization that, despite its misogynist foundation, overcomes *man's* self-estrangement. Rather than identifying himself as an object of consciousness for others, in his erotic attachment to the civic community man "transports the self into a common unity [*moi commun*] so that each citizen is no longer sensitive except in the whole" (iv 249). By so embracing his identity as part of the social whole, the citizen externalizes his inner will as the general will and thereby appears to dissolve the problem of self-estrangement that Rousseau examined in his first written work.

And yet, in the end, although Rousseau might have gone far to resolve the problem he raised in *Narcisse*, there nevertheless may be a deeper problem of narcissism echoed in his political theory. In my estimation, Rousseau constructs a vision of political community that is like a circle of mirrors in which each citizen sees only an image of himself in the eyes of all others, recognizes only his own inner will in the general will, and thus determines the laws of the state as an external expression of his own inner determination. No doubt such political purity overcomes the problem of imitating an "alien" exterior by externalizing an inner will that is not one's own. Indeed, in Rousseau's civic community, it would be difficult to find an "alien" object to internalize. In this way, the citizen overcomes the problem of the Other by seeing all others as a reflection of himself.

Rousseau's claims for harmony are predicated on the belief that social conflict arises as a result of men's identification with their private interests, wills, and desires. If they could but relinquish their particularity, he believes, they would *ex hypothesi* come to see with clarity and perspicuity the will of the community as a whole. In this respect, he maintains, particularity is the primary obstacle to political purity. But if some conflicts are in fact due to the exertion of private interest motivated by *amour propre*, certainly we must hesitate before we accept the assumption that all conflicts that threaten social harmony are attributable to such causes. For even though it eliminates such particularity, Rousseau's conception of political harmony may itself be problematic.

As does Plato in portraying Socrates' antitragic political art, Rousseau, in asserting an essential compatibility of all "desirable" ideas, values, and goods, systematically devalues all difference and particularity in constructing his own city of words. By so devaluing difference, he shapes his community into a harmonious whole—a whole that could dispel difference without moral loss. On this basis, he does not feel compelled to confront the plausible claim that, in principle, goods conflict by their very nature and that there may be no incontestable scheme for harmonizing them.[18] Rousseau can thus avoid addressing the not uncommon moral experience in which individuals are forced to choose between different moral requirements or ways of life that come into conflict.

In trying to evade these claims and conflicts, however, Rousseau embraces a theoretical position predicated on the principles of domination and inner destruction. Once each individual "puts his person and all his powers under the supreme direction of the general will" and becomes "an indivisible part of the whole," the citizen's will becomes the sole basis for moral significance (iii 361). In this regard, Rousseau valorizes the ontological status of the citizen's identity. But as the "untrammeled whole" is created from the citizens' collective will, those ethical considerations excluded from the will of the community systematically lose their ontological and moral basis.

To put it in linguistic terms, the act of subsuming particulars under a general concept is based on an abstract resemblance between particulars. Indeed, in examining the linguistic origin of general concepts, Rousseau argues that "particulars could be organized under common and generic denominations only through linguistic abstraction" (iii 149f.). As Paul de Man suggests, conceptualization for Rousseau is therefore metaphorical, "an exchange or substitute of properties on the basis of resemblance."[19] Rousseau's concept of the *volonté générale* may be understood as such a metaphor. In constructing the general will as a moral concept, however, Rousseau attempts to conceal from recognition the particularity that ineluctably forms the initial basis of his concept. Indeed, as the uncorrupt analogue of the *volonté de tous* (summation of particular wills), the "metaphor" of the general will must leave out of account the elements of difference that distinguish particulars from one another. In this way, such differences constitute the domain of "non-identity" that remains outside the structure of signification.

That which is left out in the formation of the unity of social consciousness is thus left devoid of meaning, for the structure of signification is based on the citizen's social identity. Since all value in Rousseau's state is derived from the inner depth and reality of this communal identity, all moral claims that are not reflected in the citizen's will are subject to be silenced without loss. There can be no sense of loss because, by definition, such claims have no meaning or reality. They lack the value, both ontological and moral, that is contained only within the soul of the citizen himself.

For this reason, Rousseau could avoid moral conflict only by eradicating the moral significance of conflicting differences. No doubt his concern to erase from consciousness the moral impact of these differences was based on his fear that their continued existence would ignite *amour propre*. However, his desire to exclude from consideration the ethical meaning of such differences actually reveals the inner domination that his vision of social harmony conceals from itself. Yet despite Rousseau's concealment, it is not difficult to uncover the traces of the inner domination that remain hidden in his political vision.

Indeed, to see this inner domination, we need only look to Rousseau's simple three-step argument for gender subjugation. First, unlike Socrates who at least argued for the equality of natural excellence in relation to the genders, Rousseau begins by essentializing sexual difference. On this essentialist basis, he then contentiously associates women with the home. Finally, he devalues the realm of the *oikos* in securing the ethical status of the *polis*. In these three easy steps, he sublimates and effaces women's identity as moral agents. In his state, women act only to reinforce the essential identity of men as citizens belonging to the *moi commun*. Residing outside the realm of moral signification, they are constrained to relinquish their own ethical voice and power. In this respect, women's ethical status is reduced to protecting the sanctity of men's political souls. By effacing themselves, women thus serve only to purify the male citizens' identity and will.

But though the result of establishing such purity may be that each citizen sees only his own will reflected in the single harmonious will of the community, by dissolving moral differences in regard to our complex visions of the good life and our multiple spheres of ethical engagement, Rousseau's politics collapses into a politics of narcissism. By reflecting only itself in itself, Rousseau's state is forced to turn in on itself. And just as in Hegel's description of the beautiful soul, by turning in on itself to reflect itself, "its light dies away within it, and it vanishes like a shapeless vapour that melts into air."[20]

Notes

1. Jean-Jacques Rousseau, *Oeuvres Complètes*, ed. B. Gagnebin and M. Raymond (Paris: Gallimard, 1959-1969), iv 323. Cited in this chapter and thoughout this work with volume and page number.

2. Almost immediately after *Narcisse* closed, Rousseau went to his publisher. On his own recommendation, two editions of *Narcisse* appeared in Paris before the end of the year. For the details of this event, see Maurice Cranston, *Jean-Jacques Rousseau: The Early Years* (London: Allen Lane, 1983), 287-288.

3. Cf. Joel Schwartz, *The Sexual Politics of Jean-Jacques Rousseau* (Chicago: University of Chicago Press, 1984). See my review of Schwartz's work in *Political Theory* 15 (February 1987): 138-141.

4. See Benjamin Barber and Janis Forman, "Preface to *Narcisse*," *Political Theory* 6 (November 1978): 537-554.

5. Rousseau, *Julie: ou La Nouvelle Héloïse* (Paris: Garnier, 1967), 252. Cited in this chapter as *Julie*.

6. See Rousseau's early interpretation of Plato's artistic criticism in "De l'imitation théâtrale," in *Oeuvres* (Paris: Armand-Aubrée, 1832), tome 2, 2-20. Rather than being merely three removes from the kingdom of truth, Rousseau claims, mimetic art lies four removes from this kingdom.

7. Rousseau, *Lettre à M. d'Alembert*, in *Politics and the Arts*, trans. Allan Bloom (Ithaca, N.Y.: Cornell University Press, 1960), 79. Throughout the text, this translation will be referred to as *PA*.

8. See Hans-Georg Gadamer, *Dialogue and Dialectic: Eight Hermeneutical Studies on Plato*, trans. P. C. Smith (New Haven: Yale University Press, 1980), ch. 3 (*passim*).

9. For a similar account of the mirror imagery in Rousseau see J. Starobinski, *L'Oeil vivant* (Paris: Gallimard, 1961), 93-188. See also: Walter Kerr, *Tragedy and Comedy* (London: Bodley Head, 1967), 263-309.

10. St. Augustine, *Confessions*, x.vi. For a development of this theme, see John Freccero, "Autobiography and Narrative," in *Reconstructing Individualism*, ed. Thomas C. Heller, David E. Wellbery, and Morton Sosna (Stanford: Stanford University Press, 1986), 16-30. See also Paul de Man, "The Rhetoric of Temporality," in *Interpretation: Theory and Practice*, ed. Charles S. Singleton (Baltimore: Johns Hopkins University Press, 1969), 173-207.

11. See Friedrich Nietzsche's remark concerning Schiller's conception of the "naive artist" in relation to Rousseau in *Die Geburt der Tragödie aus dem Geiste der Musik* in *Nietzsche Werke*, ed. Giorgio Colli and Mazzino Montinari (Berlin: Walter de Gruyter, 1972), Band 3(i), 33.

12. Jacques Derrida, *De la grammatologie* (Paris: Editions de Minuit, 1967), 250.

13. See John Charvet's discussion of *amour propre* in his essay, "Individual Identity and Social Consciousness in Rousseau's Philosophy," in *Hobbes and Rousseau*, ed. Maurice Cranston and R.S. Peters (New York: Anchor Books, 1972), 462-484.

14. Cf. G.W.F. Hegel's distinction between the infinite as determinate and as unbounded in *Wissenschaft der Logik* in *Sämtliche Werke*, ed. Georg Lasson (Leipzig: Felix Meiner, 1928), Band 3, 132-140.

15. See Paul de Man, *Allegories of Reading* (New Haven: Yale University Press, 1979), 139-144.

16. Georges Poulet, *Studies in Human Time*, trans. Elliott Coleman (Baltimore: Johns Hopkins University Press, 1956), 162.

17. Mikhail Bakhtin, *Rabelais and His World*, trans. Helene Iswolsky (Cambridge, Mass: MIT Press, 1965), 7.

18. See Bernard Williams's introduction to Isaiah Berlin, *Concepts and Categories* (London: Penguin, 1981), xvi-xvii.

19. De Man, *Allegories of Reading*, 146.

20. G.W.F. Hegel, *Phänomenologie des Geistes* in *Sämtliche Werke*, ed. Georg Lasson (Leipzig: Felix Meiner, 1928), Band 2, 462.

PART TWO

The Politics of Tragedy

3
A Dialogue on Liberty and Freedom

Prologue: Inside Cervantes' Archives

"Frankly, I would have wished to present this work to you naked and unadorned, without the ornament of a prologue or the countless train of customary sonnets, epigrams and eulogies it is the fashion to place at the beginnings of books." This is Miguel de Cervantes' attitude toward prologues. And I certainly understand what he means. But there is a fundamental difference between a prologue to a novel and a preface to a piece in political theory. For earnest readers trying to keep up with "the literature" in a field, a preface can serve an important economic function: It saves all but those really interested in the details of an argument the need to continue to read beyond it. By setting the stage for the story that is about to be told, a prologue, on the other hand, must invite its readers to stay.

In the prologue to *Don Quixote* we discover that the story Cervantes tells is allegedly written by Cide Hamete Benengeli. It is Benengeli's history that he is retelling. Unfortunately, Cervantes is not always in possession of Benengeli's complete manuscript. For this reason, he is often forced to leave the text of *Don Quixote* in order to find or clarify a portion of Benengeli's history. In fact, Cervantes departs from the story for months at a time. When he returns, he rarely makes excuses. He acts as if nothing transpired during the time he was away. For example, just after having been defeated by the giant windmills, in part 1 chapter 8 of Cervantes' masterpiece, Quixote is embattled with a Basque whom he takes to be an enchanter. After considerable verbal bantering, Quixote draws his sword and attacks his adversary declaring that he will soon chop him into two. Bewildered, the Basque shields himself with his pillow, brandishes his own weapon, and waits for the attack. Just when their swords are about to clash, Cervantes interrupts. With some regret, he reports that the author of this story has left the battle in suspense at this crucial point. Without providing a resolution to the episode, he informs us, the manuscript abruptly ends. Unwilling to consign the fate of Quixote to such eternal suspension, Cervantes promises that he will search the archives to find out how this battle concludes.

Following Cervantes, I too will be speaking about a battle suspended, a conflict between our demand for democratic freedom and public participation, on the one hand, and our desire to protect the liberty of the individual, on the other. This battle is fundamental to an understanding of the history and drama of modern constitutional politics. And, like Cervantes, I have also searched and re-searched for an ending. In the stories political theorists have traditionally told, I found not one, but three different conclusions to this conflict. Each of these endings follows the basic dramatic patterns associated with comedy, satire, and romance, respectively. Before I explore these endings, it is important to clarify the nature of the conflict at issue.

Observing the tension between freedom as democratic self-rule and individual liberty, Isaiah Berlin has noted that

> the desire to be governed by myself, or at any rate to participate in the process by which my life is to be controlled . . . may be as deep a wish as that of a free area of action, and perhaps historically older. But it is not a desire for the same thing. So different is it, indeed, as to have led in the end to the great clash of ideologies that dominates our world.[1]

For Berlin, the distinction between democratic freedom and individual liberty is one example of a more general division between what he has notoriously called "negative" and "positive" liberty.[2] Those who advocate "positive" liberty construe freedom as a moral project that can be achieved only if individuals govern their actions in obedience to a set of particular moral laws, ends, or goals. Along with psychic self-mastery, democratic self-government is said to belong to this group. In contrast, as a "negative" form, individual liberty requires the existence of a guaranteed area of action within which persons are free to choose their life and their ends for themselves without interference or constraint by others.

Translated into dramatic terms, the tension between democratic freedom and individual liberty may well signal a tragic condition inherent in our constitutional history. In his influential lecture on Hegel's aesthetics, A. C. Bradley captured this sense of tragedy when he said:

> It will be agreed that in all tragedy there is some sort of conflict —conflict of feelings, modes of thought, desires, wills, purpose; conflict of persons with one another, or with circumstances, or with themselves; one, several, or all of these kinds of conflict as the case may be. . . . The essentially tragic fact is the self-division and intestinal warfare of the ethical substance, not so much the war of good with evil as the war of good with good.[3]

It is to such a tragic confrontation of freedom and liberty that I now turn. Because the French Revolution is often seen as opening the threshold of modern politics, it seems like an appropriate place to begin. Just as we tend to believe that there is a harmonic structure unifying the values of liberty, equality, and fraternity proclaimed by the revolution, so democratic freedom and individual liberty have often been seen as harmonious and unified components of modern constitutional politics. Questioning an initial acceptance of this presumption, consider the conflict of liberty and freedom that emerges in the respective political writings of Benjamin Constant and Jean-Jacques Rousseau. Although Rousseau was earlier criticized for his narcissistic tendencies, to place his notions in opposition to Constant's theory is to trigger a "tragic" battle between two visions of liberty and freedom set within two different historical and political traditions.

The Battle of the Books

Jean-Jacques Rousseau was a small "r" republican.[4] What he wanted to know was: Who controls the power of the state and to whose benefit is that power to be used? His answer was that citizens must collectively control state power to their collective benefit. Rousseau regarded as despotic any regime that did not allow for the collective self-determination of its citizens. Regardless of how many individual rights they enjoy in a society, if they do not determine the laws for themselves, Rousseau believed, they live under a condition of despotism and slavery.

In contrast, Benjamin Constant was concerned with the small "l" liberal question: What constitutes the proper limits of state power and what guarantees are there that such limits will be preserved? His response was that there exists a determinate area that must remain beyond the competence and control of political authority, an area within which individuals are free to pursue their own ends without interference. Constant defined as despotic any form of political society that does not guarantee an individual's liberty. To protect this area of liberty, he argued for constitutional guarantees for individual rights, opportunities, and civil liberties.

Jonathan Swift described the war waged on that fateful Friday in King James's library almost a century earlier. Just so, in the works of Rousseau and Constant, the conflict of liberty and freedom is fought as a war between the ancients and the moderns. In Constant, we find a champion of individual liberty, an advocate of limited sovereignty, and an admirer of modern commercial society. In Rousseau, on the other hand, we find a theorist of absolute sovereignty, a proponent of political freedom, and a critic of modern society.

Constant on Ancient and Modern Liberty

According to Constant, it was common at the end of the eighteenth century for authors to imitate the virtues of the ancients.[5] Of all those who imitated ancient liberty, Constant concentrated on Rousseau. In his interpretation of Rousseau's *Social Contract*, he posed a rather interesting question: What would happen, he asked, if Rousseau's conception of liberty (appropriate to ancient society) was applied to modern conditions? Throughout all Constant's works his answer was the same: Rousseau's theory would result in political tyranny. In his *Principes de politique*, for example, Constant maintained that "the *Social Contract*, so often invoked in favor of liberty, is the most terrible support of all kinds of despotism" (272). Again, in his essay, "De l'esprit de conquete," he reiterated his opinion that the "subtle metaphysics of the *Social Contract* is only capable in our days of furnishing the arms and pretexts for all genres of despotism" (186). And in his essay on ancient and modern liberty, Constant again set out to demonstrate that "the most illustrious philosophical system of Jean-Jacques transported in our modern times would furnish the most terrible pretext for tyranny" (503).

Constant never argued that Rousseau had himself advocated a despotic form of government. Rather, he argued that Rousseau's philosophical system (his key definitions and concepts) furnished a pretext for despotism in the modern age. Constant repeatedly tells us that he did not want to join those detractors who turned Rousseau into a theorist of revolution or tyranny.[6] He believed that the goal of Rousseau, "who imitated the ancients, was noble and generous" (502). But in the hands of the Revolutionary Terror and the supporters of Napoleon, Constant claimed, Rousseau's philosophy provided a justification for the "infinite misery" and "odious measures of tyranny" endured under these regimes.[7]

Why did Constant believe that Rousseau's ancient conception of freedom was so dangerous to the modern age? To answer this question, we must place Rousseau's idea of freedom within the context of Constant's sociological analysis. Following Germaine de Staël's pioneering work on cultural comparison, Constant's analysis began as an attempt to articulate the social structures associated with a set of historical models of society. On the basis of these models, he went on to relate particular versions of political and ethical concepts to the social structures under which they could be institutionally supported. The main methodological premise underlying Constant's work is that ethical ideas and political choices are constrained by the historical development of social conditions and institutions within which these ideas and choices are to be enforced.[8] In other words, Constant argued, social conditions limit the political choices and ethical standards appropriate to a particular historical epoch.

For however much we might wish to praise the political and ethical life found at other times in other cultural epochs, according to Constant, such forms of life could not be won within the limits set by the present. Indeed, as a corollary to his sociological theory, he claimed that the ethical standards and political choices of one historical age are inappropriate and often dangerous when applied to the social conditions of another period.

Throughout his work, Constant was most concerned with identifying and justifying the ethical conceptions of liberty and freedom that correspond to the social conditions of ancient and modern societies. In specific reference to Rousseau, Constant claimed that it was no mere coincidence that the conception of moral freedom found in the *Social Contract* embraced many of the themes found in the ancient conception of political freedom. In Constant's view, ancient freedom was based on an idea of collective self-determination and an understanding of the citizen's identity as inseparably bound to the community as a whole. In his words, it consisted in

> the collective, but direct exercise of many aspects of sovereignty, deliberating in a public place on everything from war and peace to forming foreign alliances, voting on laws, pronouncing judgments, examining the accounts, the arts and the management of magistrates—making them appear before all the people to accuse, condemn or absolve them. This, which the ancients called liberty, completely joined the individual to the authority of the whole. (495)

Among the social conditions of the polis that could lend institutional support to this ancient conception of political freedom,

Constant included (1) the *size* of the polis as a small face-to-face community; (2) the *homogeneity* of the community, which provided a tradition of shared values and expectations; (3) the *political economy* of ancient life based on war and institutionalized slavery; (4) the *complexity* of the social order with its simple division of labor and relatively equal distribution of property among the citizenry; and (5) the *political organization* of public life founded on a conception of absolute sovereignty.

In contrast to the ancient conception of freedom set within the social organization of the polis was a conception of liberty appropriate to modern social conditions. In Constant's terms, "true modern liberty is individual liberty" (509). It is predicated on the claim that "there is a part of life which necessarily remains personal and independent, which rightly is beyond the competence of society" (271). Individuals in modern society "possess rights independently of all social or political authority. These rights include: freedom of person, opinion, worship, property, and against arbitrary authority" (275). Such rights may be classified as civil liberties—individuals' liberty to pursue and define their ends for themselves without interference by others. In addition, individuals have the right to influence the administration of government through the nomination of functionaries and representatives (495).

In Constant's view, this conception of individual liberty is "at home" in the large, heterogeneous, complex conditions of modern society based upon a developing commercial economy and supported by a political organization of limited sovereignty. Indeed, Constant argued, individual liberty is the only conception of liberty or freedom that can be institutionally enforced under these conditions. But he did not end his analysis with this correspondence between the sociological conditions of the modern age and the ethical status of individual liberty. Rather, he went on to warn of the dangers of imitating ancient freedom in the modern world.

"In sacrificing private independence," he declared, "the ancients sacrificed less in obtaining more; we, on the other hand, would sacrifice more in obtaining less if we imitated ancient liberty" (502). By imitating the ancients we would sacrifice our individual liberty and find ourselves subjugated to political tyranny (119). Hence, "the grand sacrifices . . . brought about naturally by the austere republicans of antiquity [in our day] would serve as a pretext for the wild unchaining of egoistic passions and tyranny" (194).

In "De l'esprit de l'usurpation," Constant argued that the fundamental principle of all forms of despotism is arbitrary political power (197). In modern society arbitrary political power is characterized by "unlimited sovereignty," that is, a conception of sovereignty that does not admit of fundamental individual rights beyond its competence to control or abrogate:

> If one does not declare that there are some objects over which the legislators do not have the right to make a law, or in other words, that the sovereignty is limited and that there are some wills that neither the people nor their delegates have the right to have, then the sovereignty must be declared an agent of despotism. (65)

For Constant, "the eternal principle which it is necessary for all modern governments to obey is the limitation of sovereignty through constitutional guarantees of individual rights" (65 n.). In his view, absolute and unlimited sovereignty forms the foundation of despotism, whether "exercised in the name of one or of all men" (202).

From this perspective, Rousseau's political society must be considered "despotic," for it does not provide a constitutional guarantee for the rights and liberties of the individual. In Constant's words, Rousseau had "mistaken liberty for authority" (188); he had committed "the error of those who, sincere in their love of freedom, attributed unlimited power to the sovereign people" (199). For this reason, "Rousseau had failed to recognize that even if absolute political authority was placed in the hands of all citizens, it was, nevertheless, absolute and despotic." As Constant wrote, "Sovereignty can be only limited and relative. At the point where personal independence and life begin, the jurisdiction of the sovereign ceases. If society goes beyond this point, it is as guilty as the despot whose only title is the sword of the destroyer" (200). In the name of ancient freedom, Constant proclaimed, Rousseau's philosophy, based on a conception of unlimited sovereignty, could thus be used as a justification for modern despotism.

Moreover, Constant found despotic implications in Rousseau's insistence that all citizens, as members of the sovereign power, must directly participate in legislative activity. Indeed, in no place is the overwhelming authority of Rousseau's state more evident than in his claim that the collectivity may force its citizens to be free. To force individuals to act in accordance with a specific goal—even if that goal is as noble as political participation—is to deprive them of their freedom. Although one may want to appeal or persuade individuals to accept their civic duty to participate in government, one can never force them to be politically free, for by the very act of compelling citizens to participate, one would deny them their liberty to define their own ends without interference or constraint. Thus, Rousseau's dictum "*on le force d'ère libre*" ("one can be forced to be free") does not reveal a paradox but a simple and dangerous contradiction that would act to force its members to participate in a despotic political system.

Not only could Rousseau's theory provide a justification for modern despotism, Constant argued, it could also furnish a pretext for the usurpation of political power in the modern state. Despotism restricts the outward forms of the individual's activity, but usurpation involves the conquest of the interior of the individual's conscience. "In a word, despotism reigns by silence and allows man the right to remain still. Usurpation condemns him to speak, it pursues him into the sanctity of his thought, and by forcing him to lie to his conscience, deprives him of the only consolation that remains to the oppressed" (172). Hence, to ensure its power, usurpation "counterfeits freedom" whereas despotism "exacts only obedience" (174).

For Constant, usurpation is implicit in Rousseau's political theory on two different levels. Recall Rousseau's division between sovereignty (the legislative power of the community) and government (the regime responsible for the execution of laws). In terms of the former, Constant claimed, by submerging the individual's identity with the community as a whole, each citizen (as a member of the sovereign power) would learn to speak only in the univocal language of the general will. In turn, the citizenry would then *willingly* relinquish its power by delegating it to the government. Because the power of the government is thereby consecrated by the free volition of the sovereign power, individuals would act to legitimate the usurpation of their own usurped power. Citizens would thus both sacrifice their own conscience to the community as a whole and then relinquish their power to a government that would use the "name of all" to justify the subjugation of all. In this double respect, Rousseau's citizens would condemn themselves "to speak only the words which express their submission to the power of the state" (172).

In addition to fearing its usurpatory and despotic qualities, Constant believed that Rousseau's *Social Contract* would create the conditions of social uniformity in the modern age. In entering Rousseau's social contract, individuals give themselves entirely to the community, creating what Constant called "an immense social power" (221). Of course, Constant recognized that Rousseau wanted to revive the strong sense of communal solidarity that characterized ancient society. But when adapted to the conditions of the modern world, he claimed, Rousseau's theory would lead to a form of social organization based on "mechanical uniformity," that is, the uniformity of individuals' identities as indivisible parts of the "machinery" of the state. In Constant's view, by making its members dependent on the institutions of state power for their own self-conceptions, Rousseau's social contract characterized the spirit of the empire—the unquestioning obedience of Bonaparte's ministers, the well-oiled machinery of his centralized bureaucracy, and the dull conformity of the people at his command.

Through the influence of Germaine de Staël, Constant was inspired instead by the expressivist goals of such thinkers as Wilhelm von Humboldt. Like Humboldt, urging a minimalist state, Constant believed that individual self-expression and self-realization could develop in a multiplicity of ways, creating a social union of complexity and rich diversification. In contrast, Rousseau's conception of the citizen, based on the principle of communal solidarity, would not only inhibit personal growth but would endanger human liberty because it would ensure that individuals would be denied any possibility of identifying themselves and their ends in their own way. By submerging their identity with the community as a whole, such individuals would be left with no other possibility than to choose the ends the state prescribes. To have only one choice is not to choose but to be forced to submit to a life in which individuals exercise no choice over their goals.

In sum, Constant declared that under modern social conditions, individuals in a state modeled after Rousseau's theory would be deprived of their liberty at every avenue, leaving them no place to turn. Politically, the state would force its citizens to choose the single path of public service. And socially, human beings would be deprived of any meaningful conception of individual liberty. No doubt it is true that individuals, as subjects of Rousseau's state, may be at liberty to pursue their particular ends as long as they do not transgress the laws emanating from the general will. But they have no rights that are beyond the jurisdiction of the state—that are protected from the state's authority. According to Rousseau's theory, the state can interfere and constrain an individual's activity in the most private of matters. And to whom do individuals complain if their personal liberty is threatened? Who else but the state. So though it is the state that deprives its subjects of their liberty, it is also the state to whom individuals must complain of such deprivation. Thus, in Rousseau's theory, individuals have no recourse against the power of the state's authority—no constitutional limits, no guarantees, no protected rights.

Benjamin Constant put these rather common liberal complaints into a more sophisticated form when he concluded that Rousseau's conception of political liberty, appropriate to the social conditions of the ancients, could provide only a pretext for tyranny when applied to the modern age. In this way, rather than a vision of true human freedom, Rousseau's portrait of society provides modern thought with a model of tyranny and despotism.

Rousseau's Defense of Political Liberty

On one point Rousseau and Constant could undoubtedly agree. Although appropriate to the social conditions of the ancients, political freedom could not be institutionally supported in modern European polities. In this respect, Rousseau would not have denied that his theory was inspired in large measure by the ancients. Raising Sparta and Rome alongside the Swiss canton as paradigmatic of institutional conditions that nurture political freedom,[9] Rousseau was not oblivious to the differences between the order he commended and the prevailing conditions he berated. He needed no reminder that his conception of moral freedom was unsuitable to the climate of existing conditions, for it was precisely in response to those conditions that Rousseau wrote the *Social Contract*. With the heterogeneous and complex world he saw emerging, Rousseau knew that there was very little room to support a small, face-to-face community in which citizens share a common past, common traditions and customs, and a common identity based on their membership in the community as a whole. Thus Rousseau did not delude himself into believing that collective self-determination and communal solidarity were suitable to the social structure and conditions of the modern age.[10]

But if in principle Rousseau would agree with Constant that political freedom could not be institutionally enforced under prevailing conditions, he would disagree with Constant's conclusion that one therefore ought to accept individual liberty as that ethical idea appropriate to the conditions of the modern age. For Rousseau, it would be a mistake to accept Constant's claim that ethical ideas can be assessed in reference to the sociological conditions of the prevailing order. Rather, Rousseau believed, the obverse is true: Prevailing social conditions ought to be assessed in reference to the demands of moral freedom. From his own assessment, Rousseau sadly concluded, true human freedom may not be possible in the modern age.

Just as their respective inferences regarding the prospect of modern liberty fundamentally differ, so do their respective attitudes toward political representation. For Constant, the right to representation was an essential part of modern individual liberty.[11] The representative system allowed individuals more time to pursue their private interests. According to Constant, "the more time and energy man dedicated to the exercise" of direct political participation in ancient society, "the freer he thought himself; on the other hand, in accord with the species of liberty of which we are susceptible, the more time for our private interests, the more will liberty be precious to us" (512). Hence, Constant declared the need for a representative system that discharges to a few individuals those responsibilities of the state that individuals either cannot or do not wish to take upon themselves. Such a system makes liberty more precious by allowing individuals to occupy themselves with the affairs of their own commerce and self-development (513).

Constant's support of the modern "virtues" of commerce is well known. "Commerce is the true life of nations," he tells us. "They want repose, and with repose comfort, and as a source of comfort, industry. It inspires in men a vivid love of individual independence. It supplies their needs, satisfies their desire," and brings to the modern age tranquility, cessation of war, wealth, and private happiness (499f.). Once again defending the idea of the minimal state, he claimed, "every time collective power wishes to meddle with private speculations, it harasses the speculators. Every time governments pretend to do our own business, they do it more incompetently and expensively than we would" (500).

As that which upholds the "virtues" of commerce and the minimal state, representation, for Rousseau, was nothing more than a system that legitimates the liberty of possessive individualism: the right of individuals to glut their souls on their own banal pleasures. "It is the bustle of commerce, the avid interest in profit, the love of commodities that transforms personal service into money," Rousseau proclaimed. "The cooling-off of patriotism, the activity of private interest, the vastness of states, the abuse of government—all these have suggested the expedient of having representatives of the people in the assemblies of the nation." Under such a representative system, "the people believes itself to be free; it is gravely mistaken; it is free only during elections; as soon as the members are elected, it is enslaved; it is nothing" (iii 429f.).

To be free is to have power to collectively control one's common destiny. The system of representation denies such power. Even Constant was forced to admit that in the modern age individuals will always "form an imperceptible element in the social will" (499). They can have little valence in terms of their relationship to the collective control of the power of the state. Concerned with the issue of power, Rousseau thus defined as despotic any form of political regime that transgressed the ancient principle of virtue as the collective self-determination of the citizenry.

Against Rousseau's definition of despotism, Constant argued that to force citizens to participate would be tantamount to denying them their liberty to define their own ends without interference or constraint. In the latter's defense, however, it should be noted that Rousseau never advocated the idea that a citizen could be compelled to participate in legislation. Rather, his notorious remark, "*one le force d'être libre*" refers to the legitimate capacity of the state to use its coercive power to force its subjects to obey the law. In this respect, Rousseau's state would hold what Max Weber was to call a "monopoly of legitimate violence."[12] It is clear that the right of the state to use coercion to enforce its laws is accepted not only by Rousseau but by Constant as well.

Moreover, in the *Social Contract*, the citizens' obligation to participate is based on their consent to the conditions establishing political society. By an act of their "free will" as an expression of their self-mastery, individuals give their consent to the social contract which, in accordance with its terms, obligates them to participate in legislation. Now, if an individual refuses to participate, that person would thereby relinquish the duties necessary to attain moral freedom. In Rousseau's view, a state in which such refusal to participate is widespread is in a state of inevitable decline and corruption (iii 135).

Besides, it was not the deprivation of a people's civil liberties but the loss of their public life that led to the tyranny of the modern age. Without the firm commitments and ties to the community in which they live, Rousseau declared, modern individuals increasingly become part of a society in which "everyone thinks of his own interests, and no one of the common good" and in which "the interests of the individuals are always opposed to one another" (ii 234). Absorbed in their private interests, they become increasingly withdrawn from the sphere of politics. They no longer identify themselves as citizens; that is, they do not identify *with* others but in *separation* from others.[13] Consequently, Rousseau felt, they lose all the commitment and ties that membership in politics implies. Above all, they lose a relationship to the *patria*.

For his part, Constant recognized that without the particular traditions of a land, individuals, "lost in unnatural isolation, strangers to the place of their birth, out of touch with the past, living in a hurried present, thrown like atoms on an immense and level plain, are detached from a fatherland nowhere visible to them, from the whole to which they grow indifferent because their affection can settle on none of its parts" (150f.). Further describing the dangers of individual isolation in modern society, he wrote: "Absorbed by the enjoyment of our private independence and in pursuit of our particular interest, we renounce too easily our right to participate in political power" (512f.). Thus, like Rousseau, Constant believed that the loss of public life breeds a sense of individual isolation.

But, unlike Rousseau, Constant warned that individuals must not sacrifice themselves and their liberty to the political state. The danger to liberty would be far greater, he argued, if in the modern age, human beings identified themselves as inseparably bound to the fatherland. In his view, submerging the individual with the state would result in social uniformity. Individuals would become nothing more than invisible parts of the state's machinery. As a condition of the social contract, they would be forced to place their ends and goals "under the supreme direction of the general will." The inevitable outcome of such a state of affairs would be the loss of individual liberty.

In Rousseau's view, however, it is not the human commitment to a political life but the institutions supporting individual liberty that create the conditions for social uniformity and the loss of human freedom. For under these conditions, Rousseau believed, human beings, possessed by *amour propre*, learn to identify themselves in terms of how they are judged and understood by others. Inseparably bound to their status as objects of consciousness for others, "a vile and deceptive uniformity" insinuates itself into modern society where "all souls seem to have been cast in the same mold" (iii 37f.). "Just as clocks are ordinarily wound up to go only 24 hours at a time," Rousseau tells us, "so these people have to go into society every night to learn what they are going to think the next day" (ii 234).

And yet Constant contends that these modern individuals are free to identify themselves—to play the parts in the performance of their private lives that they choose for themselves. On the contrary, Rousseau exclaimed: "Today, there are no longer any Frenchmen, Germans, Spaniards or even Englishmen, there are only Europeans. All have the same tastes, the same passions, the same manners for no one has been shaped along national lines by peculiar institutions. All in the same circumstances will do the same things" (iii 960).

"You might think," Rousseau declared, "that these isolated people living independently would at least have minds of their own. Not at all; they are machines that don't think for themselves, but are set in motion by springs" (ii 234). Individual liberty does not allow individuals to identify themselves and their ends in their own ways. Rather, the institutions that support such independence create the conditions for the tyranny of modern society over the individual—a tyranny that deprives human beings of their capacity and power to define their identity and ends for themselves. In the end, without a firm foundation upon which to identify themselves, modern individuals both lose their attachments to the life of the community as a whole and, in their isolated independence, fall victim to *amour propre*.

From their own weakness and dependence, such individuals feel a constant need to affirm their self-esteem. For Rousseau, the most common way human beings affirm their esteem is to appear superior to others. Thus possessed by *amour propre*, individuals are constantly thrown into an agonistic struggle for social recognition: "*Amour propre*, which compares, is never content and cannot be because this sentiment, in preferring ourselves to others, also demands that others prefer us to themselves, which is impossible" (iv 322).

In Rousseau's view, the externalization of *amour propre* helps to explain the growth of social stratification and inequality in modern society. For example, he argued that under the conditions generated by *amour propre*, private property and wealth become socially recognizable symbols of human self-esteem because they are quantifiable means by which individuals can judge one another's relative worth. Because *amour propre* leads one to dominate others so as not to be dominated oneself, private property becomes a battlefield of competition, and civil society itself becomes a war of all against all. According to Rousseau, the modern state mediates this war by establishing a basis of "legitimacy" that institutionalizes the inequality of rich over poor found in civil society. In the end, he saw in modern social conditions a vision of social oppression and the formation of government as a conspiracy of the rich. It is certainly not a vision of human freedom. The poor are dominated and enslaved by the rich, and the rich in turn are impoverished and enslaved through their own insecurities and their need to dominate others.[14]

In the *Social Contract*, Rousseau attempted to define the institutional conditions that would overcome the failings of modern society. In order to overcome the internal estrangement and external oppression inherent in the psychic and social dynamics of *amour propre*, he believed, human beings must both express their freedom as collective self-determination and understand themselves in terms of the principles of communal solidarity. And yet he was aware that his vision of freedom and communal solidarity was predicated on its own impossibility. Inspired by the ancients, Rousseau's vision of the civic community was not a blueprint of the future. Rather, it was a portrait of human freedom drawn in sharp contrast to the tyranny of the modern age.

In the end, Constant concluded that the *Social Contract* creates a pretext for a tyranny that allows the sovereignty of the people to exist as long as the people themselves do not demand their individual liberty. For his part, Rousseau would find within Constant's minimal conception of the state a form of despotism in which modern individuals relinquish their power to define their social and political lives, a tyranny in which they are guaranteed their rights to individual liberty and representation as long as they do not demand their moral freedom—their obedience to laws they prescribe to themselves. At the end of the conflict between Constant and Rousseau, we find ourselves confronted by two opposing but nevertheless compelling conceptions of the good. Poised between the value of individual liberty and the demands of political freedom, we may thus experience the self-division and intestinal warfare that Bradley described in Hegel's philosophy as the "essential fact" of tragedy. In coming to terms with this battle, as we are about to see, Hegel himself offers a comic ending to the conflict of liberty and freedom.

Notes

1. Isaiah Berlin, "Two Concepts of Liberty," in *Four Essays on Liberty* (New York: Oxford University Press, 1969), 130-131.

2. Over the years, Berlin's distinction between "positive" and "negative" liberty has been criticized by a number of formidable commentators. For example, see Gerald C. MacCallum, Jr., "Negative and Positive Freedom," *The Philosophical Review* 76 (July 1976): 312-335, and Charles Taylor, "What's Wrong with Negative Liberty?" in *The Idea of Freedom*, ed. Alan Ryan (Oxford: Oxford University Press, 1979), 175-193.

3. A. C. Bradley, *Oxford Lectures on Poetry* (Oxford: Oxford University Press, 1950), 70. Note that, correctly following Hegel, Bradley asserts the existence of an identifiable ethical substance in virtue of which opposing moral claims find their essential unity. For a critical analysis of this assertion, see Chapter 4 below.

4. Of course, as the literature in current American political theory suggests, *republicanism* and *democracy* are both disputed terms. Nevertheless, few would dispute that Rousseau defined his own republican posture in terms of the question that follows. See my remarks in Chapter 6 below.

5. See Benjamin Constant, "De l'esprit de l'usurpation," in *De la liberté chez les modernes* (Paris: Pluriel, 1980). All references to Constant are from his political essays collected in this volume.

6. Constant, "De l'esprit de l'usurpation," 186 n.3; Constant, *Principes de politique*, 272 n.4.

7. Constant, "De la liberté des anciens," 493, 502; Constant, "De l'esprit de l'usurpation," 178, 187-90.

8. On this point, see L.A. Seidentop, "Two Liberal Traditions," in Ryan, *Idea of Freedom*, 169-174; and Stephen Holmes, "Aristippus in and out of Athens," *American Political Science Review* 73 (March 1979): 113-129.

9. For Rousseau's theoretical articulation of the conditions necessary for the existence of freedom, see Judith Shklar, *Men and Citizens* (Cambridge: Cambridge University Press, 1969), 1-33; and Benjamin Barber, *The Death of Communal Liberty* (Princeton, N.J.: Princeton University Press, 1974).

10. See *Social Contract*, bk. 2, ch. 10: "In Europe, there is perhaps one country still capable of legislation; it is the island of Corsica. I have the feeling that some day this little island will astound Europe" (iii 391). Although this remark led an influential Corsican to ask Rousseau's opinion on a constitution for the island, its prophetic quality must have struck Constant--for it was from Corsica that Napoleon led his campaign to conquer Europe.

11. On the issue of popular sovereignty, it should be noted that Constant was not always consistent. Consider, for example, his role in the Cent-Jours. During the Hundred Days, Napoleon attempted to rescue his regime by offering constitutional concessions to his liberal opponents. Facing the lack of other promising political alternatives and drawn by the appeal of Bonaparte's proposal, Constant accepted a post as state adviser under the emperor. On 22 April 1815, he proposed his "*act additionnel*." This act, known as the "Benjamine," attempted to secure civil liberties within a structure of constitutional monarchy. It did not, however, significantly attempt to extend popular sovereignty beyond the purview of large landowners. For this reason, many of the liberals of his day attacked Constant for offering little more than a constitutional justification for Napoleon's power. Indeed, given his former hostility to the emperor, it seems that there was very little "constant in the Benjamine." In his *Mémoires sur les Cent-Jours*, however, Constant emphasized the consistency of his actions. He claimed that, though critical of Napoleon's regime, he was nevertheless working in the cause of the progression toward full

individual liberty (including universal suffrage and the right to representation).

12. Max Weber, "Politik als Beruf," in *Gesammelte Politische Schriften*, ed. Johannes Winckelmann (Tübingen: J. C. B. Mohr, 1971), 506.

13. For Rousseau, as for Marx in the next century, individual liberty "is a question of the liberty of man conceived as an isolated monad withdrawn into himself As a right, it is not founded upon the relations between man and man, but rather on the separation of man from man. It is the right of such separation: The right of the circumscribed individual, withdrawn into himself." *Die Judenfrage*, in Karl Marx, Friedrich Engels, *Historisch-kritische Gesamtausgable [MEGA]*, ed. David Rjazanov (Berlin: Marx-Engels Verlag, 1932), Band I/i, 593-94.

14. See Hegel's master-slave dialectic in *Phänomenologie des Geistes*, in *Sämtliche Werke*, ed. Johannes Hoffmeister, Band 2, 141f.

4

Hegelian Harmony and the Laughter of Angels

In the works of G.W.F. Hegel, the comic tradition of Western political and philosophical thought undoubtedly reaches its zenith. Like Dante in his *Divine Comedy*, Hegel offers us a daring philosophical odyssey predicated on the principles of unity, harmony, and synchronicity. The development from conflict to unity is the most fundamental structural feature of comedy as both Dante and Hegel came to understand it. They both tell a story of the reconciliation of the forces at play in the social, natural, and spiritual realms. Yet for all the similarities contained within the narrative structure of their works, there are some rather obvious differences between the "comedy" associated with the *Commedia* and the "comic" themes articulated in Hegel's philosophy.

First, although there is a good deal that is "comedic" in the *Divine Comedy*, as anyone who has tried to read Hegel knows, there is very little funny in his philosophical works. Although it is admittedly rare to find someone chuckling over the *Inferno*, no one without a very peculiar sense of humor would find anything to laugh about in the *Phenomenology*.[1] Second, philosophers like Hegel rarely employ the low style of language associated with Dante's remark that his entire work is a comedy because its language is "careless and lowly, being the speech of the common (vulgar) crowd, in which even ignorant women [*mulierculae*] converse."[2] In contrast, Hegel generally adopts a distinctly "high mimetic" mode: a structure of language pure and untainted by *vulgari eloquentia*.[3] Third, the literary genre of comedy (or even the more specific form of the *commedia*) would clearly have much too elliptical a meaning if we were to associate the prolix constructions of Hegel's teutonic philosophical style with the elegance of Dante's *terza rima*. And finally, although few could make Dante appear philosophically modest, in contrast to the Florentine poet's more personal pilgrimage to the universal, Hegel's journey encompasses nothing less than the spiritual odyssey of all of reality itself. In his work, we are presented with the journey of *Geist* (Spirit/Mind) as it comes to know itself in determinate reality.

Geist may be understood as the inner depth and rationality that pervades all of reality. In the *Phenomenology*, Hegel traced the transformation and development of diverse forms of consciousness as an articulation of the subjective journey of *Geist*. Similarly, in the *Philosophy of Right*, he articulated the development of fundamental changes in the forms of the institutional conditions of the ethical world that reflect the inner vitality and intelligibility of what he called "objective spirit."

In both its subjective and objective moments, such fundamental changes are immanent in the developmental structure of *Geist* itself; that is, they proceed by a dialectical logic of inner contradiction. The dialectic begins with a simple and immediate unity that undergoes inner division and diremption. The opposition revealed through this inner division is ultimately sublated such that a new organic whole is achieved. In turn, this unity undergoes further diremptions as *Geist* unfolds in both its subjective and objective aspects.

For Hegel, destruction is a necessary moment in the organic realization of *Geist*. Such destruction, he tells us, ineluctably results from the inner division of *Geist* itself. Indeed, in Hegel's theory, the negation of this opposition provides the basis for the creation of new forms of consciousness and reality. He described this movement as the "negation of the negation." Put in conceptual terms, *Geist* is said "first to disclose itself, then to posit the Other in opposition to itself (the negation), and finally to take (the Other) back again into itself as the negation of the negation."[4]

Of course it is important to remember that to sublate (overcome dialectically) is not to annihilate. In Hegel's words: "What is sublated is not thereby reduced to nothing. . . . To sublate has a two-fold meaning in the language: on the one hand, it means to preserve, to maintain, and equally, it also means to cause to cease, to put an end to. . . . In this way, what is overcome is at the same time preserved. It has lost its immediacy only, but it is not on that account annihilated."[5] Hence, that which is negated is not completely annihilated; rather, that which is rational is preserved in the formation of new mediated forms of subjective and objective unity. Having preserved that which is rational in the Other, the dialectical resolution of the inner division of *Geist* must contain both itself and its Other in itself.

Hegel's dialectical logic of preservation and annihilation, of creation and destruction, is reflected in his definition of classical tragedy. Recall Hegel's claim that there are three fundamental movements inherent in the narrative structure of classical tragedy. First, tragic characters are said to embody a single ethical power. Such characters

> are what they can and must be in accordance with their essential nature, not an ensemble of qualities separately developed epically in various ways; on the contrary, even if they are living and individual themselves, they are simply the one power dominating their own specific character; for, in accordance with their own individuality, they have inseparably identified themselves with some single particular [ethical power].[6]

Initially, these characters exist in simple harmony with one another. In terms of his dialectical method, we are thus presented with an initial idea of unity in its immediacy. For Hegel, the inner division of such simple unity reveals a structure of opposition. Similarly, in the course of the tragic action of dramatic works, he argued, opposing ethical powers come into conflict and contradiction:

> Everything that forces its way into the objective and real world is subject to the principle of particularization; consequently the ethical powers, just like the agents, are differentiated in their domain and their individual appearance. Now if, as dramatic

poetry requires, these thus differentiated powers are summoned into appearance as active and are actualized as the specific aim of a human "pathos" which passes over into action, then their harmony is canceled and they come on the scene in opposition to one another in reciprocal independence. (*LA* II.1196)

When taken independently, these opposing forces are equally justifiable. Indeed, "the original essence of tragedy," Hegel tells us, "consists in the fact that within such a conflict each of the opposed sides, if taken by itself, has justification; however, each can establish the true and positive content of its own aim and character only by denying and infringing the equally justified power of the Other" (*LA* II.1196). In its ethical orientation, the inner diremption experienced in the dialectical movement of tragedy thus leads to an "unresolved contradiction" in which each side contains elements of ethical validity. (*LA* II.1197).

Explicitly connecting his dialectical vision of reality with his understanding of tragedy, he argued that just as in the case of classical tragedies, "in the real world such unresolved contradictions also appear" (*LA* II.1197). And, just as the dialectical movements of *Geist* manifest in the ethical life of a community "cannot maintain such contradictions as the substance of reality and what is genuinely true," so "the proper claim of tragedy is satisfied only when it is annulled as a contradiction." Indeed, "however justified the tragic character and his aim, however necessary the tragic collision," he tells us:

> the third thing required is the tragic resolution of this conflict. By this means eternal justice is exercised on individuals and their aims in the sense that it restores the substance and unity of ethical life with the downfall of the individual who has disturbed its peace. For although the characters have a purpose which is valid in itself, they carry it out in tragedy only by pursuing it one-sidedly and so contradicting and infringing someone else's purpose. (*LA* II.1197)

Hegel's demand for tragic resolution once again mirrors his dialectical method. The negation of the negation and the force of destruction inherent in each moment of creation brings forth, as we have seen, a new mediated unity—a unity that contains both itself and its Other in itself. This vision of unity found at the very heart of his logic and manifest in his understanding of tragedy ultimately reveals the central spirit of Hegel's "divine" comedy.

Yet there seems to be an elemental tension in Hegel's theory between his use of the language of tragedy and that of comic finality. Although the former denies the philosopher access to any single principle, privileged perspective, or final vocabulary that would, once and for all, eliminate ethical conflict, the latter paradoxically requires Hegel himself to strike just such a note of finality at the conclusion of each tragic episode of *Geist's* journey. But, as Hegel understood, the dialectical movement of *Geist* is one in which comic harmonies are always seen as temporary stopping grounds, pauses between tragic disruptions on what Robert Solomon calls, "the highway of despair."[7] As one more temporary rest area on the never-ending "spiritual highway" of *Geist's* journey, Hegel offered a comic ending to the conflict of liberty and freedom.

Reconsidering the Conflict of Liberty and Freedom

If individuals wish to preserve the primacy of their natural liberty, Rousseau warned, they cannot live in civil association. If, on the other hand, they accept the duties of citizenship, they must relinquish their independence and particularity. In his judgment, there can be no third alternative. Indeed, in the *Émile*, Rousseau proclaimed,

> he who in the civil order wants to preserve the primacy of the sentiments of nature does not know what he wants. Always in contradiction with himself, always floating between his inclinations and his duties, he will never be either man or citizen. He will be good neither for himself nor for others. He will be

one of these men of our days: a Frenchman, an Englishman, a bourgeois. He will be nothing. (iv 249f.)

Unlike Rousseau, Hegel believed there was a third alternative, a conception of the state that would overcome the contradiction Rousseau had exposed. Before analyzing Hegel's own "comic" resolution to this problem, the third movement of his dialectic, we must examine his understanding of the conflict of liberty and freedom at issue. When considered independently, he believed, the liberal claims for individual liberty and Rousseau's demand for moral and political freedom "have a purpose which is valid in itself" (*LA* II.1196). However, in the tragic conflict between these two concepts, each pursues its claim "one-sidedly," thereby leading to contradiction and mutual infringement.

According to Hegel, "the merit of Rousseau's contribution to the philosophical science of the state" consisted in his argument that "adduced the will as the principle of the state."[8] Rousseau maintained that the state could be justified only on the basis of the human will and that the human will could be realized only within the state.[9] Although Rousseau was correct in demonstrating these fundamental connections, Hegel claimed, he was incorrect in identifying the proper basis of the will. Rousseau argued that the general will of the community provided "the ultimate foundation" and "absolute justification" of the state, whereas Hegel argued that the rational will of *Geist* must be seen as the state's ultimate and absolute source.

In his philosophy of the state, Hegel attempted to identify, clarify, and codify that *Geist* of rationality upon which existing social and political institutions are grounded. In contrast, Rousseau's conception of the state was drawn in direct opposition to existing institutions. In this respect, Hegel believed, it could provide only an abstract ideal [*sollen*]—a never-ending ought-to-be—that could never grasp the true rationality of the state.

In the *Philosophy of Right*, Hegel defined rationality as the "thorough going unity of the universal and particular" (258). In the state, the rational will consists in the identity that unites the will in its universality and in its particularity: "Rationality in the . . . state consists . . . in the unity of objective freedom (i.e., freedom of the universal or substantive will) and subjective freedom (i.e., freedom of everyone in his knowing and in his volition of particular ends)" (*PR* 258). In Hegel's view, the institutional structures of the modern state create the conditions for the unity of objective and subjective freedom and liberty. In other words, under the conditions of the modern state, individuals have the capacity to define themselves both in their particularity and in their universality. By thus uniting the desires of the individual with the demands of the community, he declared, the modern state had experienced its epiphany in world history.[10]

By stressing only one side of this condition of freedom and liberty, however, Rousseau failed to overcome the tragic structure inherent in the collision of these two principles. For Hegel, the one-sided orientation of Rousseau's theory is expressed both in his concept of identity based on the principle of communal solidarity and in his understanding of freedom as collective self-determination. In the first instance, Hegel claimed, the concept of identity must contain both itself and its Other in itself. In other words, we must incorporate the Other's view of us in the formation of our identity. To put it in terms of Rousseau's philosophy, we cannot base our self-conceptions either on *amour de soi* (simple self-reflection) or *amour propre* (the reflection of others).

This aspect of consciousness is explored in the opening line of Hegel's famous master-slave dialectic:[11] "Self-consciousness exists in and for itself," Hegel tells us, "when, and by the fact that, it so exists for another; that is, it exists only in being acknowledged."[12] In the context of the *Phenomenology*, Hegel's analysis is dedicated to demonstrating that a social context and ontology is necessary for a coherent conception of self-identity. Because Rousseau's conception of *amour de soi* incorporates the idea of the absolute existence of the individual's identity outside such a context, it fails as a proper basis for self-consciousness. In other words, even the notion of self-certainty that *amour de soi* expresses requires social recognition. Rousseau's understanding of *amour de soi* is thus one-sided insofar as it emphasizes only one's being "in-itself." Yet his conception of *amour propre* is equally one-sided. In Hegel's terms, it stresses being "for-itself" without being "in-itself." By judging ourselves in terms of how others judge us, we lose our self-certainty and become mere objects of consciousness for others.

Although Rousseau was certainly aware of the estrangement implicit in *amour propre*, Hegel was critical of his claim that in order to overcome self-estrangement in a political context, individuals must identify themselves in accord with the principle of communal solidarity. For Hegel, human beings are not so weak that they need choose between identifying themselves solely in terms of either the state or the judgment of others. Indeed, the claim that if individuals do not identify themselves entirely with Rousseau's community, they will identify themselves solely in terms of the judgment of others (1) severely reduces the complex social interactions within which individuals attain their self-conception and (2) thereby overestimates the obstacles to the realization of human freedom and liberty defined in terms of the individual's ability for self-definition in modern society.

In analyzing Rousseau's vision of human freedom as collective self-identity, Hegel once again criticized the one-sidedness of his position. In Hegel's view, Rousseau's description of the subjective identification of the individual as inseparably linked with the community as a whole was abstract in the sense that as a pure ideal (*sollen*) it had no external complement in the actual world. However, if one attempted to apply Rousseau's ideal to the real world, Hegel declared, the results would be disastrous. Such an attempt would produce a state that would act to eradicate all difference and particularity. Indeed, Hegel believed that the Revolutionary Terror was an attempt to bring Rousseau's "ideal" down to earth—an attempt both to eradicate all difference within the will of the community and all particularity within the structure of the state. Thus, in the *Philosophy of Right*, Hegel wrote: "When [Rousseau's] abstract conclusions came into power, they offered for the first time in human history the prodigious spectacle of the overthrow of the constitution of a great actual state and its complete reconstruction *ab initio* on the basis of pure thought alone" (*PR* 258). On the basis of Rousseau's thought, the Revolutionaries' "experiment ended in the maximum of frightfulness and terror" (*PR* 258). In his discussion of "absolute freedom" in the *Phenomenology*, Hegel examined the implications of Rousseau's conception of freedom when understood in terms of the Revolutionary Terror.

In place of the ancien régime, Hegel argued, the Revolutionary Terror hoped to create a perfect society through an act of the common will (*PH* 355). Through their common action, all citizens were gradually to become conscious of the unity of their individual will with the general will of the state. For Hegel, the consciousness of this unity expresses the consciousness of what he called "absolute freedom," which "comes into existence in such a way that each individual's consciousness raises itself out of its allotted sphere, no longer finds its essence and its work in the particular sphere, but grasps . . . all spheres as the essence of this general will" (*PH* 357).

Once each individual "puts his person and all his powers under the supreme direction of the general will" and becomes "an indivisible part of the whole," the infinite power of each individual's will becomes the absolute power of a freedom without obstacles in either the real or supersensible world (*PH* 356). Absolute freedom recognizes no significant reality outside itself. Its will is not burdened even by the will of others, for it is the general will and hence the consciousness of the unity of the will of all others. Reality stretches before absolute freedom as a realm of neutral objects that can be molded and shaped in accordance with its will, for absolute freedom is the consciousness of itself as the essence of all reality. In Hegel's words, "the world is for absolute freedom simply its own will, and this is a general will" (*PH* 356).

As the general will is brought into consciousness, absolute freedom cannot tolerate social differentiation, for it is the will of an undifferentiated whole: "Its will is the self-conscious essence of each and every personality, so that each, undivided from the whole, always does everything, and what appears as done by the whole is the direct and conscious deed of each" (*PH* 357). All forms of social differentiation are therefore seen as obstacles to the will of absolute freedom and must be destroyed for it "can let nothing break loose to become a free object standing over against it" (*PH* 358). As a result, "all social groups or classes are abolished" (*PH* 357). These social groups and classes . . . are viewed as factions that prevent the general expression of the will of absolute freedom. The social organization of France, which was traditionally based on classes and estates, therefore collapsed under the power of absolute freedom (*PH* 357).

Just as it cannot allow any division within the state, neither can it allow individuals to alienate (*derelinquere*) themselves from the state. As Rousseau put it: "The sovereignty, being only the exercise of the general will can never be alienated, and the sovereign, which is only a collective being, can only be represented by itself" (iii 368). As an indivisible part of the "collective being" of the sovereign, each individual must directly participate in legislation. These individuals can be represented neither by proxy nor by the mere "idea" of their consent to the laws. Bearing Rousseau's theory in mind, Hegel argued that the will of absolute freedom is a single (actual) will composed of the unity of all wills: "Before the general will can perform a deed it must concentrate itself into the One individuality and put at the head an individual self-consciousness" (*PH* 359). For Hegel, such collective self-consciousness is radically incoherent insofar as it denies the existence of an Other outside of itself. Without recognition of this Other, as we have seen, the collective will of Rousseau's community inevitably collapses in on itself.

In tracing the inner logic of destruction implicit in Rousseau's idea of freedom, Hegel began by examining the claim that as the single will of the community's self-consciousness, the general will must represent only itself in the process of legislation:

> Neither by the mere idea of obedience to self-given laws, which would assign to it only a part of the whole, nor by its being represented in law-making and general action, does self-consciousness let itself be cheated out of reality, the reality of itself making the law and accomplishing, not a particular work, but the general work itself. For where the self is merely represented and is present only as an idea, there it is not actual; where it is represented by proxy, it is not. (*PH* 359)

Because each is an indivisible part of the unity of all wills, individuals may not alienate themselves from the single will of the state. According to the logic of the Terror, those individuals who persist in identifying themselves with their particular wills rather than with the general will must be destroyed. By separating themselves from the single self-conscious will of the state, they become an obstacle to the will of absolute freedom. Conceiving of itself solely as a general will, the will of absolute freedom must destroy all particularity. Through the destruction of the particular, Hegel laconically noted, "absolute freedom has thus removed the antithesis between the general and the individual will" (*PH* 363).

In the execution of the will of absolute freedom, there is very little drama in putting to death those individuals who identify themselves with their particular wills. By separating themselves from the social whole, they lose their worth as human beings, for their value is acquired only in their relationship to the whole (iv 249). As discrete individuals with particular wills, they need not be treated with respect as ends in themselves. They can therefore be destroyed without hesitation because they possess no more intrinsic value than any other neutral object of nature. Once their worth as human beings is lost, they can be put to death "with no more significance than cutting off a head of cabbage or swallowing a mouthful of water" (*PH* 360).

According to Hegel, the law expressed by the general will can be actualized only through the execution of the law; that is, the law expressed in a general form is given content by those empowered by the government to apply the law to the conditions of reality. The government as the executive power (iii 395) "is itself nothing else but the self-established focus, or the individuality, of the general will" (*PH* 360).

As individuality, the government executes the law from a single point of view. Consequently, Hegel claimed, the government is merely a faction empowered with the entire force of the state (*PH* 360). Because the government defines the actual content of the general will, those who oppose its policies are viewed as "harboring particularity." Any opposition to the state must therefore be destroyed. The general will requires that all citizens will the actions of the state, therefore it is a crime to oppose the state's actions even as a "personal" act of conscience. To identify oneself with one's personal conscience is to alienate oneself from the state. Because such alienation can be hidden in the individual's inner will, the executive power of the state views all its subjects as potential enemies. Under such a regime, no one is safe from the terror of death. Indeed, referring to the famous *loi des suspects* of the Revolutionary Terror, Hegel tells us, "to be suspect has the significance and effect of being guilty" (*PH* 360).

In the end, "the unity of the will of the citizenry in the general will of the sovereign" appears to the executive power as an aggregation of particular wills. At the same time, the executive power itself is a particular will (faction) that claims generality for itself. The result is that the general will of the executive power attempts to destroy the particularity it suspects lies hidden in the sovereign, and the general will of the sovereign attempts to overthrow that which it considers the particular will of the executive power (*PH* 360). Whichever way one looks at it, Hegel concluded, the Terror could only produce destruction.

In this fashion, what Rousseau brought into consciousness—a conception of the state based on the idea of the general will—embodied in practice those principles of the Revolution that ended in terror and destruction. For Hegel, Rousseau's most fundamental and tragic error was to deny the sanctity of the "particular." That is, he criticized Rousseau's theory for depriving individuals of the expression of their particular wills—their individual liberty.

Nevertheless, Hegel agreed with many of the arguments Rousseau directed against those who one-sidedly emphasize individual liberty to the exclusion of moral and political freedom. For example, Hegel claimed that if individuals do not identify with the universal will of the state, the state itself becomes something "alien" [*fremd*] to them. In his terms, individuals are alienated from the state when they do not recognize the essence of their will in the Identity (the dialectical unity) embodied by the universal will of the state. By seeing this universal will as something Other than their own will, individuals experience their alienation as the loss of self-recognition or self-identity in the process of externalizing themselves in society (*PH* 480).

Without identifying with the universal will of the state, individuals increasingly "live outside of themselves." Indeed, for Hegel, a society of such individuals constitutes nothing more than "a sheer multiplicity of personal atoms" who define themselves in relation to each other exclusively in terms of their legal status and rights (*PH* 481). In his view, such rights remain "abstract" in the sense that they do not accrue to individuals as determinate citizens of a state. In this way, the condition of the state is equally "alien to them and soulless as well" (*PH* 481). Without identifying themselves as citizens, such individuals are no doubt free to glut their souls with their own petty and banal interests and focus their attention exclusively on their private pursuits of happiness (*PH* 481). Indeed, if individuals have no other relation to the state than the simple protection of their liberty to pursue their private interests, then they "exclude any continuity with others from the rigid unyieldingness of their atomicity" (*PH* 482). As soulless creatures within a soulless world, they thus live for nothing greater than the self-consuming pleasure of their own private ends.

In Hegel's view, those liberals who advocate such a view make the fundamental mistake of confusing the state with civil society, thereby endorsing "personal freedom as the ultimate end of association" and viewing "membership in the state as something optional" (*PR* 179). For both Hegel and Rousseau, however, "the state's relationship to the individual is something quite different from this" (*PR* 258). They argued that only if individuals identify their will with the universal will of the state can they overcome their self-alienation and establish their essential unity with others.

But in order to overcome alienation, Hegel declared, one need not deny human beings the expression of their particular wills. Individuals could identify with the universal will of the state without submerging their particular will in the "universal" (general) will of the state. Indeed, he argued that the unity of the universal and the particular can be achieved only when the universal, without annulling the existence of the particular, supersedes it. Hence, on a conceptual level,

> the universal is not external to the particular and juxtaposed to it; in their opposition, it is itself the particular, it is always both itself and its Other. Similarly, the particular is particular only through contraposing itself with the universal. Now this contraposition is the negation of the particular and, therefore, its return to the universal as the negation of the negation.[13]

On an objective level, the unity of the universal and the particular is accomplished when, as subjects of the state, individuals in civil society express their particular interests but as citizens, identify with the universal interests of the state. In this way, Hegel attempted to overcome the one-sided positions proffered by both Rousseau and his liberal critics. In his own conception of the state, he thus attempted to articulate the conditions that would resolve the tragic opposition found between individual liberty and political freedom.

Hegel's Comic Ending to the Conflict

In his analysis of ethical life (*Sittlichkeit*), the third and final stage in the development of objective spirit, Hegel announced the reconciliation of freedom and liberty in its universality and particularity. Such a reconciliation no doubt marks one of the high points of his philosophical comedy. In accord with the spirit of unity and harmony, he wrote:

> The state is the actuality of concrete freedom. But concrete freedom consists in this, that personal individuality and its particular interests not only achieve their complete development and gain explicit recognition for their right . . . but for one thing they also pass over their own accord into the interests of the universal, and, for another thing, they know and will the universal. . . . The principle of modern states has prodigious strength and depth because it allows the principle of subjectivity

to progress to its culmination in the extreme of self-subsistent personal particularity, and yet at the same time brings it back to the substantive unity and so maintains this unity. (*PR* 260)

For Hegel, the structure of the modern state creates the conditions in which individuals can be "at home" with themselves as subjects in relation to civil society and as citizens in regard to the political state.

In civil society, Hegel explained, individuals express their particular wills. Indeed, "in their capacity as burghers, such individuals are considered private persons whose ends is their own interest" (*PR* 187). Constantly striving to satisfy their own "selfish ends," individuals within civil society are "free" to appropriate through their labor any and all things they define as objects of their desire (*PR* 183, 194). At this stage, civil society breaks open into a "war of all against all"; a war in which individuals have yet to grasp a conception of themselves based on the rational will. "The feeling that needs, their satisfaction, the pleasures and comforts of private life . . . are absolute ends . . . displays their lack of acquaintance with the nature of *Geist* and the end of reason" (*PR* 187). Each views the Other as something external, as an obstacle to the satisfaction of his or her particular needs and desires. In this war of all against all, "particularity by itself, given free rein in every direction to satisfy its needs, accidental, capricious and subjective desires, destroys itself . . . in the process of gratification. . . . The system of ethical order is split into its extremes and is lost" (*PR* 185-184).

However, in their struggle with others for the acquisition of such objects of desire, Hegel claimed, these individuals gradually become dependent on others for the satisfaction of their needs and desires. Hence, like Adam Smith's "invisible hand," the "cunning of reason" creates the conditions under which each person, striving for particular ends, becomes the means for the satisfaction of the ends of others (*PR* 199). "The particular person is essentially so related to other particular persons that each establishes himself and finds satisfaction by means of the others" (*PR* 182). In their relations to one another in civil society, a "form of universality" is thereby adopted: "In the source of the actual attainment of selfish ends—an attainment conditioned in this way by universality—there is formed a system of complete interdependence, wherein the livelihood, happiness, the legal status of one man is interwoven with the livelihood, happiness and rights of all" (*PR* 183).

Although their wills are universal in form, individuals in civil society still identify themselves with their own particularity: with their particular work embodied in their class, with their particular rights established in the administration of justice, and with their particular interests promoted in their corporation. At this stage, the universal interest of the whole of society is not a part of individuals' consciousness of themselves. Rather, they view such universal interest as something external to them, an obstacle to the realization of their particular wills. Thus, in civil society there remains an antagonism between private and public interest.

In Hegel's view, it is only within the state that the essential Identity between the universal and particular can finally be established. He maintained that in contrast to individuals' conception of themselves in civil society, "the state is an external necessity and . . . higher authority; its nature is such that the laws and interests (of individuals) are subordinate to it and depend on it. On the other hand, however, it is the end immanent within them, and its strength lies in the unity of its own universal end and aim with the particular interests of individuals" (*PR* 261). As indicated, in the overcoming (Aufhebung) of civil society, the state does not completely annul its existence. Rather, the "moment of particularity is itself essential to the unity found in the state", so "particular interests should not be set aside or completely suppressed; instead they should be put in correspondence with the universal, and, thereby both they and the universal are upheld" (*PR* 261).

"*Geist*," Hegel says, is found in the nature of human beings in their "explicit individuality" on one extreme and in their "universality" on the other (*PR* 264). Although "explicit individuality" can be found in civil society, it must be unified with individuals' consciousness of their interests in the universal, which can only be acquired through their membership in political institutions (*PR* 258, 264-267). On the one hand, Hegel believed these institutions would preserve and protect the particular interests of individuals in civil society. On the other hand, he claimed that through political institutions, citizens would, at the same time, identify with the universal will of the state.

Of course, unlike Rousseau, Hegel was notoriously critical of direct political participation. In his view, such a "republican" conception of "the sovereignty of the people" was based on the "wild idea" of placing a "formless mass" in charge of the state (*PR* 279). As one might suspect, rather than the undifferentiated rule of "the people," differentiation marks the set of institutions Hegel articulated. The principal features of these political institutions include: (1) a constitutional monarchy based on heredity whose function is to provide the final act of formal sanction for the policies and laws of the state; (2) an executive power composed of an extensive bureaucracy of civil servants whose class interests are identical to the interests of the whole community; and (3) a legislative assembly of estates divided according to class and concerned with the determination of laws that reconcile the interests of the state with the interest of civil society (*PR* 273). Through the combined activities of the crown, the executive, and the legislature, *Geist* is said to come to its full realization in the state (*PR* 258). And with this realization, Hegel believed, true human freedom finally became actual in the world.

In this way, Hegel concluded, meeting Rousseau's original challenge, the individual identifies himself as both a man and a citizen; his duties and his inclinations reconciled, he contributes both to the good of himself and to the good of all others. In the abstract, the individual is nothing, but as a member of the state that embodies the rational will of *Geist*, he is determinate, actual, concrete, and free.

The Laughter of Angels

Many contemporary thinkers have, of course, challenged Hegel's vision of unity. Some, like Isaiah Berlin, have argued that rather than reconciling the conflict of liberty and freedom, Hegel synecdochically places the universal over the particular, the state over the individual, and positive over negative liberty. In this way, Berlin calls into question the reductive aspects of Hegel's spirit of resolution. In his view, such resolution relies on Hegel's belief that there exists a privileged philosophical language that orders and subsumes all prior moral vocabularies; a language that can translate such vocabularies into its own terms without loss of meaning or significance. Deciphering this language, Hegel believed that he could finally, once and for all, grasp the dialectical movements of *Geist* as it had come to fully realize itself in his thoughts. In Hegel's words:

> All . . . systems of philosophy are only reflecting images of this one living being. . . . This living spiritual power moves, agitates within itself, and realizes itself in an organic system, a totality, containing a rich set of levels and aspects. At once, philosophy is the understanding of this development and this thought development itself because it is thought which understands.[14]

Employing "the vocabulary of *Geist* itself" in his conception of freedom as self-realization, Hegel thus emphasized the privileged status of the "real" over and against the merely "empirical" self. Hierarchically constructed, however, Hegel's vocabulary subordinates the claims of the latter into the language of the former. "This magical transformation or sleight of hand," Berlin maintains, is based on Hegel's conception of the self as inwardly divided. The unwarranted effect of such inner division is found in the subsequent ease with which Hegel was able to split our personality between a higher "transcendent, dominant controller" and a lower "empirical bundle of desires and passions to be disciplined and brought to heel."[15]

This same strategy of subordination and reduction occurs on a political level. There Hegel's conception of the "real" self is inflated into the super-personal entity of *Geist*. In this respect, Hegel's language of realization is not the final articulation of *Geist*. Rather *Geist* itself simply mirrors Hegel's notion of the "real" self. Like this latter conception, Hegel's positive conception of freedom as self-mastery could thus achieve its proclaimed harmony only by devaluing the content of individual liberty from the beginning. If you want to be "truly" or "really" free in Hegel's state, you must overcome your "lower," "empirical" desires of "particularity" and identify with the "higher" "more real" interests of the "universal." For Berlin, the consequences of identifying with the universal will of the state can be traced in the rise of modern totalitarian regimes.

In a very different philosophical key, Karl Marx also questioned the idea of resolution found at the end of Hegel's discussion of the state. Rather than claiming that the universal subsumes the particular, however, Marx argued that the universal serves as little more than an ideological veil for the rule of various forms of particularity within the state: the particular interests that rule the monarchy, the estates, and the bureaucracy.

To offer just one example, Marx viewed Hegel's bureaucracy as a political analogue to the civil corporation. In civil society, such corporations are universal bodies bound interdependently by the goals of particularity. Each member, motivated by particularity, aligns with the universal interest of the corporation. At the same time, the universality embodied in the corporation is defined in terms of the particular interest of its collective body. In this respect, as a kind of political corporation, the bureaucracy transforms the state's universal aims into claims of private interest on both an individual and institutional level. "For the individual bureaucrat, the end of the state becomes his private end: a pursuit of higher posts, the building of a career."[16] On a collective level, the universal interest of the state itself becomes the private interest of the bureaucracy (i.e., the state's interest in its own power). In this way, the corporation (union of interdependent private interests in civil society) acts as the civil counterpart of the bureaucracy and the bureaucracy the political counterpart of the corporation.

At the same time, however, the bureaucracy and the corporation represent opposed forms and thus constitute what Marx called a special instance of the institutionalization of the duality between the state and civil society. Exemplifying this duality in the structure of government, he claimed that as representatives in the assembly of estates, members of the landed and business classes must similtaneously identify both with their private, class interests and with the universal interests of the state. In Marx's view, such structural contradictions remain hidden beneath the surface of Hegel's vision of unity. He concluded, then that despite its claims of unity, the "essential" contradictions between *l'homme et le citoyen* on an individual level and civil society and the state on an institutional level remain unresolved in Hegel's philosophy.

Put in its most general form, "Hegel's fundamental mistake," Marx tells us, "consists in conceiving a contradiction in appearance as a unity in essence, in the Idea. But it really has something much more profound in its essence, namely an essential contradiction."[17] Rather than resolving these fundamental contradictions, he believed, Hegel's articulation of unity acted only to conceal the real forces of opposition at play in the social and political world.

For all of their obvious differences, both Marx and Berlin challenge Hegel's vision of unity. The latter says the particular is subsumed by the universal. The former says the universal is said to be consumed (but not digested) by the particular. For both, Hegel's state fails to attain the comic resolution of freedom and liberty it sought to establish.

Against the totalizing aspect of Hegel's philosophy, Milan Kundera has suggested the danger inherent in all comic attempts to overcome human tragedy:

> People have always aspired to an idyll, a garden where nightingales sing, a realm of harmony where the world does not rise up as a stranger against man nor man against other men, where the world and all its people are molded from a single stock and the fire lighting up the heavens is the fire burning in the hearts of men, where everyman is a note in a magnificent Bach fugue and anyone who refuses his note is a mere black dot, useless and meaningless, easily caught and squashed between the fingers like an insect.[18]

In Kundera's terms, the deep pleasure of ethical totality is echoed in the "serious laughter of the angels" who eternally express their unity and joy of being (233). Yet when they are fully persuaded that their thought is guided by rational necessity, this divine laughter and joy denotes the "enthusiastic laughter of angel-fanatics, who are so convinced of their world's significance that they are ready to hang anyone not sharing their joy" (233). Echoing with such divine laughter, the tradition of Western political theory has no doubt experienced its problem with angels.

Notes

1. See Dorothy Sayers, "The Comedy of the Comedy," in *Introductory Papers on Dante* (Oxford: Oxford University Press, 1956), 151-178.

2. Dante's reason for employing this style was ultimately political. He believed that using the common idiom of Italian instead of Latin would help to unify the people, providing them with a universal language of harmony shaped from their own discursive practices. *Dantis Alagherii Epistolae*, ed. Paget Toynbee (Oxford: Clarendon Press, 1966), 177.

3. Northrop Frye, *Anatomy of Criticism: Four Essays* (Princeton, N.J.: Princeton University Press, 1957), 33-71.

4. G.W.F. Hegel, *Die Wissenschaft der Logik* in *Sämtliche Werke*, ed. Georg Lasson (Leipzig: Felix Meiner, 1923), Band 4, 495.

5. Ibid., 495.

6. G.W.F. Hegel, *Lectures on Fine Arts*, trans. T. M. Knox (Oxford: Oxford University Press, 1975), II.1194. Cited below as *LA*.

7. Robert Solomon, *In the Spirit of Hegel* (Oxford: Oxford University Press, 1983), 289.

8. G.W.F. Hegel, *Philosophy of Right*, trans. T. M. Knox (Oxford: Oxford University Press, 1942), para. 258. Cited below as *PR*.

9. G.W.F. Hegel, *Vorlesungen über die Geschichte der Philosophie* in *Sämtliche Werke*, ed. Karl Michelet (Stuttgart: Friedrich Frommann Verlag, 1965), Band 19, 527-529.

10. See G.W.F. Hegel, *Vorlesungen über die Philosophie der Weltgeschichte* in *Sämtliche Werke*, ed. Georg Lasson (Leipzig: Felix Meiner, 1923), Band 9, 748.

11. The dialectical peripety Hegel examined in terms of the relation between master and slave may well have found its source and origin in Rousseau's famous declaration, "L'homme est né libre, et par-tout il est dans les fers. *Tel se croit le maître des autres, qui ne laisse pas d'être plus esclave qu'eux*" (Man was born free and everywehere he is in chains. He who believes himself to be the master of others, is a greater slave than they). (*Oeuvres complètes*, ed. B. Gagnebin and M. Raymond [Paris: Gallimard, 1959-1969], iii 351). Nevertheless, as we will see, implicit in Hegel's analysis is a criticism of Rousseau's conception of self-identity and consciousness.

12. G.W.F. Hegel, *Phenomenology of Spirit*, trans. A. V. Miller (Oxford: Oxford University Press, 1981), para. 178. Cited below as *PH*, using Miller's paragraph numbers.

13. Jean Hyppolite, *Genesis and Structure of Hegel's Phenomenology*, trans. Samuel Cherniak and John Heckman (Evanston, Ill.: Northwestern University Press, 1974), 147.

14. G.W.F. Hegel, *Vorlesungen über die Geschichte der Philosophie* in *Sämtliche Werke*, ed. Johannes Hoffmeister (Leipzig: Felix Meiner, 1938), Band 15, 27.

15. Isaiah Berlin, "Two Concepts of Liberty," in *Four Essays on Liberty* (New York: Oxford University Press, 1969), 134.

16. Karl Marx, *Kritik des Hegelschen Staatsrechts* in *Historisch-kritische Gesamtausgable* [*MEGA*], ed. David Rjazanov (Berlin: Marx-Engels Verlag, 1932), Band I (1), 507.

17. Ibid., 510.

18. Milan Kundera, *The Book of Laughter and Forgetting*, trans. Michael Henry Heim (London: Penguin, 1978), 8.

5

A Carnival of Critics: Irony and the Postmodern Temper

In thinking beyond Hegel's logic of the absolute, many in the post-Nietzschean age have offered what might be appropriately described as a satirical response to the conflict of liberty and freedom. Parasitic upon Hegel's comic resolution, satire acts to disrupt the promise of a happy ending. By disrupting the transparency of linguistic exchange that comedy seeks to establish, it achieves such disruption through parody. Indeed, such "satire gains its effect precisely by frustrating normal expectations about the kinds of [endings] provided by . . . Romance, Comedy, or Tragedy, as the case may be."[1]

Before we approach the heart of our subject, it might be wise to inspect this idea of satire more closely by illustrating it in the work of Michel Foucault. More consistently than any other postmodern thinker, Foucault has developed the implications of Nietzsche's criticism of history as totality. Against Hegel's comic finality, for instance, he proclaims, there can be no closure at the end of time that would render coherent the whole of history. "The nineteenth century is commonly thought to have discovered the historical dimension," he tells us, "but it did so only on the basis of the circle, the spatial form in which the gods manifest their arrival and flight and men manifest their return to their natural ground of finitude."[2]

In his essay "Nietzsche, Genealogy, and History," Foucault suggests that his own histories may be read as the parodic doubles of the monumental, antiquarian, and critical modalities characterized in

Nietzsche's *Untimely Mediations*.³ In Foucault's terms, as we will see, the monumental becomes farcical, the antiquarian becomes dissociative, and the critical becomes sacrificial.

Monumental history, he begins, supplies its confused and anonymous readers with alternative identities. It provides them with prototypes of greatness drawn from the past. Transposed into its satirical Other, the past in Foucault's analysis thus becomes a costume party, a display of masks and "ephemeral props" that "point to our own unreality" (*NGH* 161). As Nietzsche put it in *Beyond Good and Evil*,

> Again and again a new piece of prehistory or a foreign country is tried on, put on, taken off, packed way, and above all studied. We are the first age to have truly studied "costumes"—I mean those of moralities, articles of faith, taste in the arts, and religions—prepared like no previous age for a carnival in the grand style, for the laughter and high spirits of the most spiritual revelry, for the trancendental heights of the highest nonsense and of Aristophanean mockery of the world. Perhaps this is still where we shall discover the realm of our invention, that realm, in which we, too, can still be original, say as parodists of world-history and carnival clowns of God—perhaps even if nothing else today has any future, our laughter may yet have a future.⁴

Rather than taking such a charade seriously, Foucault joins Nietzsche in urging the historian to enjoy this masquerade by "taking up its disguises" and "revitalizing the buffoonery of history" (*NGH* 161).

In contrast to the goals of the monumental, "antiquarian history" identifies not with the unique and substantial characters of the past but with the "continuities of soil, language, and urban life in which our present is rooted" (*NGH* 162). As the parodic double of such history, Foucault's studies trace the discontinuities and heterogeneous systems dispersed in our discursive practices and cultural traditions. Exploring the ruptures, tears, gaps, and lacunae in the concrete situations of the past, his histories thus transform the integrative into the dissociative.[5]

Finally, offering a parodic double of critical history, Foucault criticizes the judgments of injustice rendered against the past in the name of scientific knowledge and truth. Such judgments, he tells us, are nothing more than "effective illusions by which humanity protects itself" (*NGH* 163). For Foucault, what is at work in discourse—as in everything else—is the play of "desire and power."[6] In order for the aims of desire and power to be realized, however, discourse must ignore its basis in them; that is, it must mask from itself the fact that it is a manifestation of them. By seeing the mask as a mask, however, Foucault's parodic double of critical history sacrifices the historian's will to knowledge. In this respect, he confronts the metaphysical basis of modern rationalism (the will to knowledge) with the question first raised by Nietzsche: "What if the equation of the divine and the true becomes less and less credible, if the only things that may still be viewed as divine are error, blindness and lies, if God himself (the truth) turns out to be our longest lie?"[7]

At the conclusion of Book V of *Thus Spoke Zarathustra*, Nietzsche's poet brings together a carnival of outcasts who perform a parodic ritual of the Last Supper. At the end of the festival the lonely poet dances with tears of joy in his eyes.[8] The significance of this festival is not only found in its obvious satirical inversion of Christian doctrine. Perhaps more importantly, it signals the end of our capacity to believe in the inherent order and ethical totality of the world. Indeed, it seems to suggest that as a culture we have failed to sustain our belief in that high spirit of comedy that experienced its epiphany in Hegel's philosophy.

Of course, Foucault is not the only postwar writer who deserves to be included in Nietzsche's carnival of critics. Jean-Paul Sartre and Jacques Derrida undoubtedly share Nietzsche's satirical posture toward the principles of comic totality. But, as we will see, if Sartre's early existential writings can be accurately described in satirical or parodic terms, Derrida's inscriptions might best be understood in terms of the art of self-parody.

Sartre's Satire

For Sartre, human reality (*Dasein*) is an impossible struggle of consciousness to attain the solidity found in the world of things. Sartre distinguishes between being *en soi* (being in itself) and being *pour soi* (being for itself) as each is translated into the elemental metaphor of *Being and Nothingness*.[9] Being in itself (*en soi*) describes being that is thinglike. Thinglike being is solid (*massif*) and unified, Sartre tells us, but it lacks consciousness. In contrast, being for itself (*pour soi*) describes the being of consciousness. In depicting this latter form of being, Sartre employs two different metaphoric strategies. He often portrays conscious being, in contrast to the stability of being *en soi*, as a shifting and flickering awareness of the world and as an alchemy of translucence and opacity. In both metaphoric strategies, Sartre represents being *pour soi* as lacking the quality of thingness.

For Sartre, "the best way to conceive of the fundamental project of human reality is to say that man is a being whose project is to be God" (*EN* IV.1.iii). It is a struggle to achieve the Totality of God, as a Being (being both in and for itself). Hence, "to be man means to reach toward being God. Or if you prefer, man fundamentally is the desire to be God" (IV.1.iii). But it is a struggle destined to failure. In the words that end the final part of *Being and Nothingness*: "Man is a useless passion" (IV.2.iii).

Always striving to be God, humans can never achieve their project. Rather, Sartre suggests, it is the very condition of freedom itself that brings upon the failure of human reality. For Sartre, freedom is strictly identified with nihilation. "The only being which can be called free," he tells us, "is the being which nihilates its being" (IV.1.iii). Defined as *le néant* that lies at the heart of Being, freedom is the creative impulse of consciousness as nihilation. On the temporal level, this nihilation is the consciousness of time. As Sartre put it in his famous line, being *pour soi* "never is what it was and never will be what it is" (IV.1.iii). It is thus the being of a "decentered" subject. In terms of its quality, he claims, the nihilating spirit of consciousness again leads being *pour soi* away from any fixed center or firm ground in which it could anchor.

To illustrate the latter point, consider the second metaphoric strategy alluded to previously in Sartre's discussion of the quality of being in *Being and Nothingness*. There, being *pour soi* is likened to the transparent *néant* of pure water that runs through a viscous and slimy stream. In his discussion of the *visqueux*, Sartre likens the project of freedom to the appropriation of honey from a jar. If I put my fingers in a jar of honey, he tells us, the pliant quality of the honey allows it to be shaped. But this very quality also prevents me from fully appropriating it according to my freedom. When I want to let go of it, it clings and lingers. "It is a soft, yielding action, a moist and feminine sucking, it lives obscurely under my fingers, and I sense it like vertigo" (III.2.iii).[10] Cast adrift in a viscous world of overdetermined meaning, being *pour soi* forever seeks to define itself in terms of its action, to shape the thick and gelatinous language of human reality into a transparent vision of its freedom.

Of course, it should be noted that Sartre is not always consistent in his use of the term *freedom*. In "L'Existentialism est un humanisme," for instance, freedom appears associated with the Kantian idea of autonomy as the identity of individuals as absolute ends capable of determining their moral actions for themselves. Throughout his early works, freedom also takes on a slightly different aesthetic quality. It is the free expression of the artistry of life, the creation of a world as a projection of one's humanity. Conversely, in *Qu'est-ce que la littérature?* Sartre claims that just as the goal of human freedom is the art of life, the goal of art is to recover the human reality of freedom.[11] Finally, in the works I will be addressing, freedom is often associated with the idea of liberation as resistance to oppression. In all its many guises, however, Sartre's idea of freedom is clearly different from either the democratic idea of collective self-determination and sovereignty or the liberal notion of individual rights and the absence of interference. And yet, as we will see, it nevertheless offers us a critical perspective from which to view the conflict of liberty and freedom.

Sartre's Satirical Ending to the Conflict

In the past, Sartre has been seen as a tragic thinker.[12] More recently, however, the self-critical, self-destructive, and even deconstructive nature of his work have been increasingly emphasized.[13] Given the deep strains of parody, mockery, and irony laced throughout his writings, this latter description does not seem out of place. Indeed, particularly in regard to Hegel, Sartre satirically deploys the themes of tragedy itself to disrupt the expectations raised in Hegel's comic ending to the conflict of liberty and freedom. Indeed, he raises Hegel's model of tragic conflict in order ultimately to defeat it.

In his 1946 essay "L'Existentialism est un humanisme," Sartre seems to offer a classic example of tragic conflict as the confrontation of dialectical opposition and contradiction. There we are presented with the case of a young man who must choose between joining the French resistance movement or protecting the safety and happiness of his mother by remaining at home. "He was faced with two very different kinds of action," Sartre writes,

> one, concrete, immediate, but concerning only one individual; the other concerned an incomparably vaster group, a national collectivity, but for that very reason was dubious, and might be interrupted en route. And, at the same time, he was wavering between two kinds of ethics. On the one hand, an ethics of sympathy, of personal devotion; on the other, a broader ethics, but one whose efficacy was more dubious. He had to choose between the two.[14]

Confronted by these two kinds of ethical action, this young man was engaged in an intestinal battle waged not between good and evil but between equally compelling but incompatible ways of life. In this respect, Sartre's student was inescapably locked in a situation of tragic conflict.

No one, Sartre tells us, could help this young man decide which alternative to follow. Christian doctrine valorizes both options with such imperatives as "'Be charitable, love your neighbor, take the more rugged path.' But which," Sartre asks, "is the more rugged path? Whom should he love as a brother? The fighting man or his mother?" (EH 25) Similarly, he claims, Kantian a priori ethics cannot be of much help. In this situation, two equally valid but incompatible moral maxims could certainly be formulated in accordance with the categorical imperative. Emotive principles are of even less use because, according to Sartre, we must be responsible for choosing our emotional orientation toward our action and ways of life.

Like Hegel, Sartre thus portrays tragedy as an ethical situation in which an individual is confronted by a stark choice between opposing poles. The classical theater faced its audience with characters who embodied contradictory ethical principles, whereas in modern tragedy, Sartre tells us, this battle of moral forces often takes place within the interior consciousness of a single individual. In terms reminiscent of Hegel's *Lectures on Fine Art*, he writes: "In ancient theater, what is interesting is that each *persona* represented only one term of the contradiction, never both. Here you have on one side the family, on the other side, the city. . . . What is new today in the theater . . . is that there are . . . contradictions interior to the character of a single individual."[15]

Following Søren Kierkegaard, however, Sartre appears to raise Hegel's understanding of tragedy only to oppose it. Unlike Hegel, in the concrete particularity of the situation, Sartre refuses to furnish a way out of tragic conflict.[16] Like the choice confronted by his student, Sartre's theater explores what he called the *universel singulier*: the concrete specificity of a situation that corresponds to a universally experienced phenomenon. Here Sartre followed Andre Gide's idea that "C'est qu'en etant le plus individuel, on est le plus universel" (in being the most individual, one is the most universal).[17] Projecting the universal in its singularity, Sartre depicted those concrete situations in which individuals must choose between equally compelling, but incompatible ways of life.

Contrasting the *universel singulier* to Hegel's idea of consciousness with its claims of unity underlying opposition, Sartre attempted to defeat the logic of dialectical sublation. Against all such abstract universalization, Sartre believed, Kierkegaard saved the value of the true, unique interiority of each individual. Moreover, "he gave the lie to the internal organization of Hegel's system," Sartre wrote, "by showing that superseded moments are conserved, not only in the *Aufhebung* that maintains them as it transforms them, but in themselves, without any transformation whatever."[18] Unmasking this lie, Sartre disrupted Hegelian dialectics by obscuring the transparency of linguistic exchange that lies at the basis of Hegel's faith in sublation. Sartre accomplished this task by posing the irreducible subjectivity of the being of the Other as that which cannot be grasped in Hegel's language of appropriation.

More specifically, he deploys this ineffable Other in a rigorous logic of dialectical suspension and negativity. Of course, it should be noted that "negativity" is not the same as "nihilation." The former is the suspension of dialectics without mediation. The latter is the very quality of the Other that disrupts our faith in Hegel's comic idea of sublation.

For example, when Sartre turns to the problem of the Other in *Being and Nothingness*, he concentrates on Hegel's master-slave dialectic. Recall that Hegel eventually attempted to overcome the problem of the Other by positing self-consciousness as both itself and its Other in itself. Rather than leading to mutuality, however, in Sartre's view, Hegel's idealism leads to epistemological and ontological optimism (*EN* III.1.iii). First, Sartre claims, Hegel optimistically assumed that the knowledge others have of us corresponds to our perception of ourselves as objects for them. Although we may recognize ourselves as objects for others, others cannot perceive us from our vantage point. For to "know" how others see us would be to "know" the Other as a free subject. But we "know" the Other only in the light of our own free subjectivity. To put it bluntly, being an object is not equivalent to being a subject. Indeed, there is an unbridgeable distance between the two. Rather than posing as an epistemological problem as it (allegedly) does in Hegel's theory, Sartre argues, this distance and gap is established by the being of the Other. In its own free subjectivity, he tells us, this being *pour soi* resists the appropriation of itself in the world.

In a related move, Sartre poses what he called the "scandal of plurality" against Hegel's ontological optimism. Hegel affirms the unity of the whole of Being, yet he merely asserts that each consciousness is a moment of the whole and that the whole is a mediator among these pluralities. Once again, Sartre's ontological criticism is predicated on the being of the Other (with its radical and irreducible subjectivity) as that which disrupts the ontological optimism contained in Hegel's idea of sublation.

Sartre emphasizes not the mutual recognition achieved in Hegel's dialectic but the mutual failure and entrapment inherent in the relation between two conscious beings. Our relations with others, he tells us, is from beginning to end a relation of frustration, constraint, and conflict: "While I attempt to free myself from the hold of the Other, the Other is trying to free himself from mine; while I seek to enslave the Other, the Other seeks to enslave me... Descriptions of concrete behavior must be seen within the perspective of conflict" (*EN*, iii.1.4). From this perspective, the Other's expectation and views of us necessarily restrict the achievement of our desire to be recognized as free. Trapped by the gaze of the Other, we are confined by the Other's perception of us. Caught peering through a keyhole, we are crystallized into the jealous, shameful creatures that the Other takes us to be. In the concise but caustic words of Sartre's satirical *Huis-clos*, "hell is other people."

Illustrating hell, Sartre ironically transports Hegel's master-slave dialectic to the battlefield of sexual behavior. There, he adopts the negative and satirical posture that love and desire ultimately lead to the bleak poles of masochism and sadism (*EN* III.iii). In the former, the failure of love is transposed into the love of failure. Sartre claims that in becoming an object of fascination for another (*en soi*), masochists, like the slave in Hegel's portrait, give up their independence as conscious beings for themselves (*pour soi*). Given the impossibility of attaining the ontological status preserved for things in the world, however, masochism fails to sustain the love for which it was willing to sacrifice itself and instead becomes fascinated with itself as an object of failure.

On the other extreme, the attempt to overcome the freedom of the other by using one's flesh as an instrument of subjugation similarly ends in failure. With one glance from the victim, the aggressor realizes that the Other still exists as an independent being. The failure of sadism thus stems from the recognition that the Other is not merely an object of consciousness but a subject. In this way, rather than achieving the fulfillment of mutuality, Sartre's dialectics of submission and domination ironically lead to negativity, the sterility of affection, and the failure of love and desire expressed in masochism and sadism. So much for love.

Of course, Sartre's parodic use of the logic of dialectical negation is not confined to the domain of the intimate. On a political level, Hegel's desire to find a resolution to the conflict of liberty and freedom similarly ends in disruption and failure. Rather than articulating within itself the unity of freedom in both its universality and particularity, Hegel's analysis is, in Sartre's hands, suspended at its most extreme point of negation without mediation.

On the side of the universal, we find the road to totalitarianism preserved. Here, in the name of the universal, human beings relinquish their independence and identify with the determinism established by the inner rationality that is said to underlie the state. From the state's perspective, individuals are perceived to be little more than objects. In their concrete behavior, Sartre argues, they only too frequently live up to the state's expectation. Indeed, he tells us, protecting themselves from the anguish of recognizing their freedom, in bad faith they reflect the status of themselves as beings *en soi*. They thus lose the self-recognition of their status as beings (*pour soi*) capable of radical projects of self-creation. For the early Sartre, such totalitarian dynamics could be found in either capitalist or communist regimes. In his view, they were both ossified forms that deadened individuals' recognition of their protean freedom.

On the side of the particular, we witness the vertiginous charm of a "bourgeois carnival" suspended in its unmediated negativity. In this procession of bad faith, Sartre claims, each participant seeks to live in the eyes of the Other. Like reflections cast in a circle of mirrors, these individuals offer a dizzying display of inauthenticity. Yet, reflected in each individual's private pursuits, what we actually see displayed in this carnival are the barren expectations and empty "values" of bourgeois culture.[19] Because money, status, power, and above all, being taken seriously are the qualities that most command respect, it is necessary for such individuals to have or at least to affect them. In this way, as in Rousseau's description of *amour propre*, individuals become trapped as objects of consciousness for others.

In his remarks on the comic actor in *L'Idiot de la famille*, Sartre illustrates this point. What the actor parodies on the comic stage is the *truth* of the bourgeois.[20] Its appearance, buffoonery, and pretense *is* its truth. Conversely, what the comic actor reveals off the stage is the negation of that which he parodies. By portraying the respectable bourgeois in everyday life, the comic actor thus betrays the truly ridiculous character from which his life is in fact drawn. "The serious is proposed, is decomposed and recomposed, only to be disintegrated once more," Sartre remarks; "being dissolves into appearance" (831). The truth revealed by the comic artist comes from the indignation incorporated in the paroxysm of our laughter: "You tried to dupe us, to get us to take you for a man, but we're not that stupid, we know you are a clown" (831). Trapped as objects of consciousness for others, in Sartre's opinion, we too are like those actors who relinquish their capacity to be other than carnival clowns. In a moment of disgust that comes from both repudiation and identification, Sartre thus wrote, "I have no longer anything to say to the bourgeois!"[21]

For Sartre, the deadening and vacuous paths of both bourgeois culture and totalitarianism lead to bad faith, bad art, and bad politics. Exploring them in their unmediated negativity, Sartre exposes what he calls "*l'esprit de sérieux*" (the spirit of bad faith) of Hegel's project. Such a spirit views human beings as objects and subordinates them to the world of *Geist*. As the "unity of Being," the articulation of *Geist* is said to express "values" that have absolute existence independent of human reality (*Dasein*). For Sartre, as we have seen, living in accordance with such values is a way to hide from, rather than to realize, freedom. Hence, in regard to the inadequacy of

Hegel's comic resolution to the conflict of liberty, Sartre tells us, the negation of the negation does not "burst our limits and become affirmation."[22] Rather, Hegel's philosophy posits only an unacceptable ideal synthesis that lies beyond the conflict, restraint, and frustration of human experience.

For all its criticism of Hegel's philosophy of the state, Sartre's early work cannot provide a positive conception of politics.[23] But perhaps we should not demand such a conception from it. As satirical, such a demand may well miss the point of his writings. Although it is true that Sartre cannot supply a reconciliation to the conflict of liberty and freedom, his early task is undoubtedly one of critical resistance and liberation. By demonstrating the failure of totality in our very pursuit of it, he places into question our illusory desire for a perfect society where complete stability combines with complete individual awareness.

In our Faustian desire to appropriate our own subjectivity, to make the world transparent to us as an image of ourselves, Sartre reminds us, we are necessarily doomed. Not only are there other Faustian creatures out there ready to disrupt our plans, but, as we saw at the beginning of our discussion of Sartre, we can never fulfill our project to become God. In this respect, human beings are destined to be failed gods: to fail at love, to fail at politics, and to fail at our most basic project in life.

Yet there is something gained through all this failure. For Sartre, to be capable of failing is unassailable proof of our freedom. Things in the world cannot fail, only conscious beings can. As Fyodor Dostoevsky shows with his underground man, the proof that one is not a "piano key" is demonstrated by one's capacity to suffer and to resist. On a political level, this paradox is expressed in Sartre's recollection of the Occupation. In the *Republic of Silence*, he speaks of a politics of liberation carved out of despair:

> We were never more free than during the German occupation. We had lost all our rights, beginning with the right to talk. . . . Because the Nazi police tried to force us to hold our tongues, every word became precious like a declaration of principle.

> Because we were hunted down, every one of our gestures had the weight of a solemn commitment... Thus the basic question of liberty was posed, and we were brought to the verge of the deepest knowledge that man can have of himself. For the secret of a man is not his Oedipus complex or his inferiority complex: it is the limit of his own liberty, his capacity for resisting torture and death.[24]

Crucial for Sartre's early theory of resistance was that so many of his fellow citizens were willing to excuse themselves from taking responsibility during the Occupation. Sartre demanded instead that in every concrete situation we choose who we are in the world. Exemplified in the choice confronted by his student, Sartre's concept of freedom requires that we activate the palpable force of our being in the world; it calls for action even within a situation of despair.

From Satire to Self-Parody

In French intellectual circles since the war, Sartre's views have often been criticized. Paradoxically, however, much of this criticism seems to draw from Sartre's own critical writings against the determinism inherent in all metaphysical conceptions of human reality. Indeed, as we have seen, it was precisely on the basis of Sartre's opposition to such conceptions that he criticized the Hegelian faith in synthesis.[25] What, then, is the significance of this repetition of criticism? Or, to put it another way, why deconstruct Sartre's critique of metaphysics? Appropriately, Jacques Derrida has posed this latter question in his essay, "Les Fins de l'homme."[26] By way of conclusion, I would like to trace the satirical quality in Derrida's reading of Sartre's reading of Heidegger's reading of Husserl's reading of Nietzsche's reading of Hegel, although not necessarily in that order.

In exploring the question of "*les fins de l'homme*" (the ends of man), Derrida examines the telos of human reality ironically endorsed by the "humanist" readings of Hegel, Husserl, and Heidegger that dominated postwar France. For Derrida, of course, such readings are ironic not only because these latter thinkers understood themselves in opposition to the "anthropological" and "anthropocentic" claims of humanism. They are also ironic because the claims of humanism were made in opposition to all telic conceptions of "human reality."

Derrida points to Jean-Paul Sartre as leading the procession of "humanists." "Even if one does not wish to summarize Sartre's thought under the slogan "'existentialism is a humanism,'" he writes, "one must recall that the major concept, the theme in the last instance, the irreducible horizon and origin was what was then called 'human reality'" (FH, 136).[27] As a misreading of Heidegger's *Dasein*, "human reality" was defined in Sartre's works as a "neutral and undetermined notion" that was substituted for the idea of the "unity of man" with all its "metaphysical heritage" (FH, 136). For Derrida, philosophers who embrace the "unity of man" are those who talk about such things as "the unity of our minds, bodies, and souls," or "the unity of the ends embedded in us by nature," or "the unity of nature embedded in our ends." Defining their writings in opposition to these ideas, humanists could neutralize the metaphysical aspirations for a determinate answer to *les fins de l'homme*. Or at least they thought they could.

However, Derrida suggests, in substituting "the unity of human reality" for the "unity of man," Sartre's philosophy (ironically) repeated the metaphysical claims it simultaneously opposed. Derrida notes, for example, that in *Being and Nothingness*, "the history of the concept of man is never examined. Everything occurs as if the sign 'man' had no origin, no historical, cultural, or linguistic limit" (FH 137). To illustrate Derrida's point, take the case of Sartre's young student. Thrown into a condition of tragic conflict, the student is told that he is radically free to choose. But from what position does he choose? For Sartre, the answer can only be that he must choose from a position outside and separate from the finitude of his situation. In this respect, in its anthropocentrism, Sartre's philosophy nevertheless sought a metaphysical position that lies beyond the confines of human reality.

According to Derrida, the ground and horizon of this metaphysical position is found in Sartre's description of "the essential project of human reality." At the end of *Being and Nothingness*, Derrida suggests, the old idea of "the unity of Being" is metaphysically transposed into the new idea of "the unity of human reality" with its project to attain the Totality of Being *pour soi* and *en soi*. In this way, Sartre's "humanism" is really just another way of talking about the ends of man in relation to God (as Totality). As Derrida puts it: "Being in-itself and Being for-itself were of Being; and this totality of beings, in which they were composed, itself was linked up to itself, relating and appearing to itself, by means of the essential project of human reality" (FH 137). At this point, Derrida's writing suspiciously breaks out into a sudden burst of clarity: "What was thereby named, in an allegedly neutral and indeterminate way, was nothing other than the metaphysical unity of man and God, the relation of man to God, the project of becoming God as the project constituting human reality" (FH 137f.).

For Derrida, Sartre's metaphysical project seems to endorse Heidegger's proposition that "every humanism remains metaphysical" (FH 138). For example, note how Sartre's ocular and tactile metaphors of being *pour soi* appear to offer only a slightly new version of the old Kantian-Fichtean-Husserlian model of the transcendental subjectivity of the constituting agent. In Sartre's version, as I mentioned earlier, the project of human reality is one that attempts to appropriate the translucent quality of one's own subjectivity by shaping the unformed being *pour soi* into a world that mirrors itself. Hence, "consciousness is not limited to projecting affective meanings onto the world around it: it lives the new world which it has just constituted" (*EN* I,i). In its purity, however, it sees both its own subjectivity and the subjectivity of the Other as the possibility of its freedom and the source of its contamination and failure. For just as the Other disrupts and frustrates our freedom, the gooey quality of our subjectivity constantly threatens to stop up the hole that lies at the heart of our being. Thus for Sartre, the deadly sweet density of consciousness sticks to the hands of the transcendental subject like language to the hands of a writer.

For thinkers like Derrida, however, Sartre's "project of human reality" is just another way of trying to gain a privileged view from which to recover the truth of the world as it really is. For Hegel, the world *really* was the expression of *Geist*, this time, it really is the arena of battle between being *pour soi* as the pure against the gooey. In the end, the difference between these two thinkers doesn't really amount to much since even in his denial, Sartre still seeks the privileged domain of the ultimate signified.

Of course, Sartre understood much of this. He understood, for example, that his philosophy was parasitic upon the very metaphysical project it opposed. Indeed, it is the inevitable failure of this metaphysical project that neutralizes and underdetermines *les fins de l'homme*. For Sartre, that is how we come to recognize both our finitude and our freedom. In this way, Sartre satirically deploys the metaphysics of failure as the failure of metaphysics to determine the project of human reality.

If Sartre knew all this, then what is the significance of Derrida's repetition of Sartre's criticism of metaphysics? Or, to ask the question again, why deconstruct Sartre's critique of the metaphysics of presence? The answer to this latter question may be found in Derrida's fascination with repetition and denial. Opposition repeats that which it denies. Such is the case even with Sartre's use of the metaphysics of failure to expose the failure of metaphysics. It cannot escape from the metaphysical position it opposes. The same is true with Heidegger. For though Heidegger was aware that humanism was parasitic on metaphysics, Derrida claims, in opposition to humanism, his own project repeats the metaphysical position it opposes. The same can be said of the critiques of anthropologism inscribed by Husserl, Nietzsche, and Hegel. They each suffer what they deny. And they each deny the metaphysics underlying the claims of humanism.

In "Les Fins de l'homme," Derrida explores the possibility of producing a kind of philosophy without a center, without a transcendental or constituting subject, and without a telos or end in light of which our projects and practices acquire their significance. In criticizing the tradition from Hegel to Sartre, he maintains that in its search for the answer to the question of Being, Western philosophy has, even in its denial, always determined Being in terms of a metaphysics of presence. As is well known, his criticism of Western metaphysics focuses on exploding the hierarchy implicit in the polarities of our discursive practices that privilege Presence, Unity, and Identity over distance, difference, and deferment. These latter terms articulate what Derrida calls the unspeakable gap of *différance*.

As the gap and distance inherent in all speech acts, *différance* inhabits the terrain of what appears to be immediate and present. The illusion of the self-presence of meaning or of consciousness is thus an impossibility: a façade and mask covering over *différance*. In therapeutic terms, Derrida's deconstructive efforts may best be described as an attempt to demonstrate the suppression of *différance* as the basis of all claims to Being and Presence, claims that are predicated on an implicit hierarchy and suppression of the Other.

In the end, Derrida confronts us with "two false exits" taken by those who attempt to escape the metaphysics of presence. The first incorporates many of the satirical gambits we have already witnessed in Sartre's early existential writings. According to Derrida, such writings are based on the decision "to attempt an exit and a deconstruction without changing ground, by implicitly repeating the founding concepts and the original problematic, by using against the edifice the instruments or stones available in the house, that is to say, in language as well" (FH 162). The problem, of course, is that by remaining on this terrain, "one risks ceaselessly confirming, consolidating, or raising [*relever*], at an always more certain depth, that which one allegedly deconstructs. The continuous process moving toward an opening through explication," he concludes, "risks sinking into the autism of the closure" (FH 162).

The second gate of ivory appears to carry us to a realm different from the one we seek to escape. It is based on the decision "to change terrain, in a discontinuous and irruptive fashion, by brutally placing oneself outside, and by affirming an absolute rupture" and *différance* (FH 162). In this respect, deconstruction plays an edifying role in its attempt to align itself with the ineffable Other that does not present itself as the negation of itself, as something that can be brought back within the presence of itself. Indeed, the only thing we can say about the Other is that we can't grasp it; it is the unspeakable, the silent.

No doubt, traces of this silence can be detected in Sartre's writing. For example, "the being which is nothing, which is not a being [etant]," he tells us, "cannot be spoken of, cannot speak itself" inside the House of Being, that is, within the domain of metaphysical language (*EN* 167). To illustrate this claim, consider Sartre's criticism of Hegel. According to Sartre, the Other always escapes Hegel's language of appropriation because it neither yearns for nor yields to but, as gap and silence, satirically ruptures dialectical sublation. In this way, Sartre's deconstruction mimes the ineffable Other as that which disrupts, interrupts and clouds the transparency of the signs exchanged. But as Derrida reminds us, the further Sartre's writing attempts to flee the terrain of dialectical sublation, the closer it approximates Hegel's ground of Being as the project of Totality. Hence, like the first exit, this strategy seems only to "ceaselessly reinstate the new terrain of the oldest ground" (FH 162f.).

In thinking beyond Hegel's logic of the absolute, both Sartre and Derrida strike a common cord of satire. Indeed, as members of Nietzsche's carnival of critics, they offer a parodic eulogy to Hegel's comic philosophy, a eulogy that resurrects the dead in order to kill it. If Sartre resurrects the idea of metaphysics only to destroy it, however, Derrida appears to resurrect his own resurrection of Sartre's resurrection of Hegel, only to once again destroy it in an endless play of *différance*. In this way, if Sartre's philosophy can be described as satire, then Derrida's may best be understood as self-parody.[28] Indeed, at the end of "Les Fins de l'homme," it is clear that Derrida is not unaware of the "style" of his own inscriptions.[29] Caught in a web of parody and self-parody, of resurrection and death, he concludes, we have not yet found the poet who could respond to Nietzsche's call for the one who "burns his text, erases the traces of his steps" and learns "to dance outside the House of Being."[30]

Notes

1. Hayden White, *Metahistory* (Baltimore: Johns Hopkins University Press, 1973), 8.
2. Michel Foucault, "The Father's No," in *Language, Counter-Memory, Practice*, trans. Donald Bouchard and Sherry Simon (Ithaca, N.Y.: Cornell University Press, 1977), 85.
3. Michel Foucault, "Nietzsche, Genealogy, History," in *Language, Counter-Memory, Practice*, 139-165; cited below as *NGH*.
4. Friedrich Nietzsche, *Beyond Good and Evil*, trans. Walter Kaufmann (New York: Vintage, 1989), no. 223.
5. Foucault rejects the claim that exclusive attention should be given to the discontinuities of history. But in tracing the discontinuities *as well as the continuities* in our cultural tradition and practice, Foucault still employs the archaeological and genealogical methods first introduced by Nietzsche.
6. Like Nietzsche, Foucault finds the operations of power dispersed throughout life in a multiplicity of shifting forms. In his view, it is a mistake to attempt to locate power in simple institutional terms. All relations are relations of power and desire that need to be analyzed in their concrete and disparate manifestations. As an example of the dispersion of power, see Foucault's remarks on the increase of power and control resulting from the "humanism" of the nineteenth-century penitentiary in *Surveiller et punir* (Paris: Gallimard, 1975).
7. Friedrich Nietzsche, *Genealogy of Morals*, trans. Walter Kaufmann (New York: Vintage, 1958), 258. On this point, see Foucault's "A Preface to Transgression," in *Language, Counter-Memory, Practice*, 30-33.
8. For an interpretation of this episode that stresses its parodic elements of style, see Gary Shapiro, *Nietzschean Narratives* (Bloomington: Indiana University Press, 1989), ch. 4.
9. Jean-Paul Sartre, *L'Être et le néant* (Paris: Gallimard, 1943); cited below as *EN*. In translating this work, I have relied on Hazel E. Barnes's edition of *Being and Nothingness* (New York: Washington Square Press, 1966).
10. On the political implications of Sartre's description of the feminine, see, for example, Jean Bethke Elshtain, *Public Man, Private Woman* (Princeton, N.J.: Princeton University Press, 1981), 306-308.
11. Jean-Paul Sartre, *Qu'est-ce que la littérature* (Paris: Gallimard, 1949), 41.
12. For example, see the classic work by Wilfrid Desan, *The Tragic Finale* (Cambridge, Mass.: Harvard University Press, 1954).

13. For example, see Christina Howells, *Sartre: The Necessity of Freedom* (Cambridge: Cambridge University Press, 1988), ch. 4.

14. Jean-Paul Sartre, "L'Existentialism est un humanisme" (Paris: Nagel, 1946), translated and edited by Bernard Frechtman and reprinted in *Existentialism and Human Emotions* (New York: Philosophical Library Press, 1957), 25. Cited below as EH.

15. Jean-Paul Sartre, *Un Théâtre de situations*, ed. Michel Contat and Michel Rybalka (Paris: Gallimard, 1973), 139.

16. Consider, for example, the contradiction found in *Les Mains sales*: "If the Party is right I am more lonely than a madman. If the Party is wrong the world is done for." Jean-Paul Sartre, *Les Mains sales* (Paris: Gallimard, 1949).

17. Quoted by Sartre in *Un Théâtre de situations*, 77.

18. Jean-Paul Sartre, "The Singular Universal," in *Between Existentialism and Marxism*, trans. John Mathews (New York: Pantheon, 1974), 148.

19. Values, Sartre insists, do not have independent status. For this reason, accepting what is considered to be valuable in bourgeois culture does not grant respectability to ethical agents. Rather, they freely choose to allow themselves to arise and become engaged in what is said to be worthy. In this way, they become invested with respectable morality by deciding to acquiesce to the blessings and taboos of their culture. See *EN* I.1.

20. See Jean-Paul Sartre, *L'Idiot de la famille* (Paris: Gallimard, 1971), I.825-831.

21. Sartre, *Un théâtre de situations*, 74. Like Flaubert's, Sartre's much-discussed relation to bourgeois culture is undoubtedly a complex one of distance and proximity, of repudiation and identification.

22. Jean-Paul Sartre, *Saint Genet, comédien et martyr* (Paris: Gallimard, 1952), 235.

23. Particularly in Anglo-Saxon literature, Sartre is frequently criticized on this basis. For example, see Mary Warnock's subtle but critical analysis of this point in *Existentialism* (Oxford: Oxford University Press, 1970), 113-141.

24. Jean-Paul Sartre, "La République du Silence," in *Situations 3* (Paris: Gallimard, 1949), 11-13.

25. On this point, see Howells, *Sartre: The Necessity of Freedom*, 194-202.

26. Jacques Derrida, "Les Fins de l'homme," in *Marges de la philosophie* (Paris: Editions de Minuit, 1972), 129-164. Cited below as FH.

27. Derrida is certainly aware of Sartre's criticism of humanism elaborated in *La Nausée*, but he relegates this criticism to a footnote. See FH, 4n.

28. For a more explicit account of what I have called Derrida's self-parody, consider his *La carte postale de Socrate à Freud et au-delà* (Paris: Aubier-Flammarion, 1980). There Derrida deconstructs his own deconstructions

of the relation between the reading of literature and the reading of life into a private communiqué of experience. On this point, see Richard Rorty, *Contingency, Irony and Solidarity* (Cambridge: Cambridge University Press, 1989), 126-137.

29. His own *style* "weaves and interlaces the two motifs of deconstruction" described as the "the two false exits" already discussed. Of course, it might be objected that by calling Derrida's a discourse of self-parody, I have neglected his endorsement of Nietzsche's claim that a change of style must be plural. But in particular regard to the idea of Totality, satire, as defined at the outset, acts to disrupt expectations of all styles. Hence, in deconstructing totalizing texts, the proliferation and dissemination of styles does not preclude the latter from being described as parodic, ironic, or satirical.

30. Nietzsche, *Beyond Good and Evil*, no. 223.

6

Arendt, Rorty, and Mr. Jefferson's American Romance

In *Federalist* 49, Publius praises Thomas Jefferson for displaying equally "a fervent attachment to republican government and an enlightened view of the dangerous propensities against which it ought to be guarded."[1] In the balance of Jefferson's writings there is no doubt a tension between his "republican" and "enlightened" views. Redescribed, such a tension may be found in terms of Jefferson's advocacy of both traditional liberal and democratic principles of politics.[2] For example, though critical of Jefferson's enlightened views, Richard Rorty has recently argued that, as the author of the Virginia Statute for Religious Freedom, Jefferson demonstrated a profound liberal concern to accommodate the plurality of moral beliefs within society.[3] Nevertheless, as Hannah Arendt reminds us, Jefferson undoubtedly held an "equally fervent attachment" to the spirit of democratic participation and local autonomy.[4] Once again, in these interpretations of Mr. Jefferson's America, we are confronted by the conflict of liberty and freedom. In what follows, I offer a final set of endings to this conflict by tracing the "romantic" elements contained in the works of Rorty and Arendt, respectively.

Romance and the Romantics

Because both authors have been critical of nineteenth-century Romanticism, it is important to clarify the elements of "romance" I will be attributing to their works. As a way of initially distinguishing between their own "romance" and the "romantic" narratives they criticize, consider the central metaphors Arendt and Rorty use in describing the Romantic poets. For example, Arendt tends to appeal to the metaphor of darkness and light to convey her criticism of the subjectivity and introspection celebrated by the Romantics.[5] Those who view the act of self-revelation as an act of introspection, she tells us, enter the "chartless darkness" of the mind and the heart, a terrain that cannot be known or brought to light.[6]

She associates politics and worldliness, in contrast, with the realm of "light and illumination." In her view, the public space of action and speech is located at the center of that realm. It is the arena within which human beings reveal themselves to others. For Arendt, the full revelation of one's being in the world requires both performance and audience. "Though disclosing itself intangibly in act and speech," she writes, the "identity of the person becomes tangible only in the story of the actor's and speaker's life" (*HC* 193). Without an audience who can bear witness to their actions and memorialize their heroic speeches and deeds, human beings, lost in their own subjectivity, will forever remain hidden both to themselves and to others. For this reason, we are told, Romantic poetry signifies nothing more than an escape from reality into "empty dreams" and "unheroic illusions."

Against this Romantic tendency, Arendt's own "romance" concentrates on the recovery of what remains lost and hidden in the modern age. In particular, she argues that by indulging in the "private" fantasies of our own subjectivity and focusing almost exclusively on the "social" domain of economic gratification, we have lost a sense of the "public" and the "political." In recovering these domains, Arendt employs the narrative form traditionally associated with "romance" as a quest. Revivifying the ideals of the past, her quest is dedicated to reasserting the importance of the political as the arena of self-disclosure and self-presentation. For Arendt, this illumination of the self takes place when we act in concert with others to determine and define a collective life. In this way, political life can be seen as the activity through which relatively large and permanent groups of a people shape their collective destiny. Within the extent of their powers, they answer what Tolstoy once described as *the* question, "the only question truly important for us: "What shall we do and how shall we live?'"[7]

In her quest to recover and bring to light "the political," Arendt draws from a number of notions central to the discursive and cultural practices of the classical age. For example, her distinction between the "public" and the "private" (or "social" in its modern connotation[8]) is based on the Greek understanding of the relationship between the household (*oikia*) and the political realm (*bios politikos*). According to Arendt, the household served predominantly economic and non-political functions. Finding its locus in the realm of necessity, it was the place of labor, the dominion of women and slaves guided and controlled by the master who depended on them to satisfy the basic needs of the family.[9]

In contrast, the polis was said to be founded on the equality of relation between citizens in terms of their admission to public life as the sphere of true freedom. It was the locus of men's struggle for self-revelation and glory. Endorsing a kind of political machismo, Arendt fills her work with recollections of the acts and speech of great men.[10] It comes as no surprise that her heroes are Homeric rather than Platonic and Roman rather than Romantic. Indeed, in contrast to what she describes as the latter's dismal flight into the internal realm of conscience, Arendt portrays Achilleus as the paradigmatic hero of the political.

The story of Achilleus, she tells us, is the story of a man willing to die rather than to suffer a dishonored memory. In that single deed he was able to sum up the "essence" of his being so that "the story of the act comes to its end together with life itself" (*HC* 194). Yet even Achilleus "remains dependent upon the storyteller, poet, or historian, without whom everything he did remains futile" (194). By raising this warrior as the paradigm of the hero, by preserving his memory in her own narration, Arendt attempts to recover the very "essence" of what it means to "win immortal fame" as a political actor.

Arendt undoubtedly offers us a "romance" of the past. Richard Rorty, however, offers us a "romance" of the future. His is a quest for alternate descriptions and redescriptions that human beings, as language users, can employ as valuable tools in constructing a better future. The hero of Rorty's narrative quest is not one whose act and speech is to be preserved immemorial but one whose very mission is to reshape the way in which we come to talk and act in the world.

"In my view," he tells us, "an ideally liberal polity would be one whose culture hero is [Harold] Bloom's 'strong poet' rather than the warrior, the priest, the sage, or the truth-seeking, 'logical,' 'objective' scientist."[11] Such a poet is "a strong maker, the person who uses words as they have never before been used" (*CIS* 28). According to Rorty, "she can see, more clearly than the continuity-seeking historian, critic, or philosopher, that her language is as contingent as her parts or her historical epoch. She can appreciate the force of the claim that 'truth is a mobile army of metaphors' because, by her own sheer strength, she has broken out of one perspective, one metaphoric, into another" (*CIS* 28).

Rorty's narrative history of culture traces the metaphoric shifts in philosophy. More ambivalent than hostile to the enterprise of Romanticism, he begins by endorsing those Romantic poets who "claimed for art the place in culture traditionally held by religion and philosophy, the place which the Enlightenment had claimed for science" (*CIS* 3). Rejecting the metaphorical foundation of scientific rationalism, Rorty continues, these artists attempted to shatter the Enlightenment's faith in Mind as a "mirror of nature," in Knowledge as the accuracy of the representations reflected in that Mirror, in Truth as the correspondence between knowledge and the world, and in Art as the imitation of the True. In subverting this picture of the world, the Romantics relied on the metaphors of consciousness rather than on those of reflection. For them, Art was not imitation but expression; consciousness was not a transparent medium of representation but a medium of human self-realization; and Truth was not to be discovered or found, it was to be created by the poet.

Rorty clearly "thinks of himself as an auxiliary to the poet rather than to the physicist," but his sympathy with the Romantics does not inhibit his criticism of them (*CIS* 8). Although Romanticism was an important stage in our narrative history, he claims that it was only the "other side" of the Enlightenment. To illustrate this point, Rorty redescribes both sides in terms of their linguistic commitments. Rather than following the Enlightenment's depiction of language as the transparent medium through which the self could come to know what lies outside it in the world, he tells us, the Romantics viewed language as the expressive medium through which the self decodes and realizes in the world that which lies within its own depths. In Rorty's view, however, "language is not a medium for either expression or representation" (*CIS* 11). Rather, he aligns his own pragmatic stance with Ludwig Wittgenstein's metaphor of alternative vocabularies as alternative tools that human beings use (*CIS* 11).

Just as Hegel believed that he had "overcome" Romantic subjectivity in his own philosophy, Rorty says the discursive practice of pragmatism in his historical narrative "overcomes" the language of Romanticism. The notion that Romantic "philosophy might replace science as a substitute for religion," Rorty maintains, "was a momentary, though important stage in the replacement of science by literature as the presiding cultural discipline."[12] However, he continues, Romanticism in turn "was *aufgehoben* in pragmatism with its claim that the significance of new vocabularies was not their ability to decode, but their mere utility" (*CP* 153). Here, of course, Rorty is not referring to Hegelian dialectics as an articulation of *Geist*, but to the success of pragmatism's redescription of the enterprise of philosophy itself.

Like the postwar authors already discussed, both Rorty and Arendt are critical of the finality with which Hegel's synthetic unity of freedom resounds. In his romance of the future, Rorty rejects the "telic" and "metaphysical" conception of freedom found in Hegel's philosophy of the state. Instead, he focuses his attention almost exclusively on the prospects of individual liberty. In contrast, Arendt rejects Hegel's valorization of the "private" and "social" domains secured through the "liberty" of civil society. In her romance of the past, she concentrates on the idea of freedom as direct participation in a political life with others.

Hannah Arendt's Romance of the Past

In the context of her "romantic" narrative, Arendt sharply distinguishes among the meanings of "liberation," "individual liberty," and "democratic freedom." In the course of her remarks on "liberation," she directly criticizes Sartre's theory. As a matter of political praxis, she tells us, Sartre's work can only too easily be used to justify unlimited violence. For example, she reminds us that in his introduction to Franz Fanon's *Wretched of the Earth*, Sartre himself had stated rather clearly that in movements of national liberation, "irrepressible violence" is fundamental to the project of "man recreating himself."[13] Recognizing the parasitic links between Sartre and Hegel, Arendt sardonically notes that at least the author of the *Philosophy of Right* believed that self-creation was simply a matter of thought (OV 115). When repeated in Sartre's theory, however, it becomes a matter of violence and "mad fury" (OV 115).

From her perspective, the flaw in Sartre's argument is apparent. In claiming that there does not exist a link between the inner worlds of individuals, Sartre falsely concludes that our confrontation with others is necessarily one of "negation" predicated upon our desire to subjugate, enslave, and torture the Other. But, as Arendt put it, "there is all the difference in the world between 'denying any link' with somebody and 'negating' his otherness; and for a sane person there is still a considerable distance to travel from this theoretical "negation" to killing, torturing, and enslaving" (OV 186). Collapsing these differences, Sartre's theory carries us closer to the proximity of such violent acts. Indeed, by urging a violent eruption of negation, his theory of liberation can lead only to destruction.

Even if it is not defined in terms of Sartre's existential project, "the notion of liberation," Arendt tells us, "can only be negative" (*OR* 29).[14] In distinguishing liberation from "the desire for freedom," she claims, "liberation may be the condition of freedom," but it cannot advance freedom itself. Rather, in modern revolutions, she reminds us, the idea of liberation has most frequently been associated with the extension of individual rights.

Here, Arendt introduces the division between individual liberty and democratic freedom. At best, movements of liberation bring about the former rather than the latter. The fruits of individual liberty are "absence of restraint and possession of the power of locomotion" (*OR* 29). Even if "constitutionally guaranteed," these individual rights remain "not powers of themselves, but merely an exemption from the abuse of power" (*OR* 151). Such liberties can be enjoyed in private isolation and can exist even in the absence of democratic institutions. Indeed, according to Arendt, they may be secured under a monarchy or in a system of feudal hierarchy, though not under tyranny or despotism (*OR* 31). Such liberty may lead to the absence of oppression, but it cannot replace the experience of freedom itself (*OR* 32).

Rather, the "actual content of freedom" is "participation in public affairs, or admission to the public realm" (*OR* 30). It requires a "political way of life," which means "the constitution of a republic" (*OR* 30). In her analysis of the founding, she persistently identifies with Jefferson's emphasis on direct participation. For example, she summarizes Jefferson's discussion of a ward system modeled after the New England township by saying that "whether Jefferson knew it or not, [the basic assumption] was that no one could be called happy without his share in public happiness, that no one could be called free without his experience in public freedom, and that no one could be called either happy or free without participating, and having a share, in public power" (*OR* 255).

Arendt's romantic elegy to the loss of political freedom in America is drawn from the republican tradition. She charts this loss, which is firmly anchored in the past, in order to gain a critical perspective from which to view the future of our liberal polity. Indeed, her romance serves as a warning against current trends toward what Alexis de Tocqueville first described as soft despotism. Like Tocqueville, she warns against the encroachment of a centralized administrative force. As Tocqueville claimed, such a force would both erode the local, participatory spirit of U.S. democracy and enhance the isolation and atomization of individuals who increasingly withdraw into themselves.[15]

In *Human Condition*, Arendt directs her criticisms against the "rise of the social," the disappearance of political life, and the atomization or privatization of the public sphere. For her, the "rise of the social" reflects our prominent concern with issues of economics, production, and necessity. Although these issues were considered private in the ancient world, they have become the central focus and preoccupation of the modern age. Large, impersonal, and bureaucratically organized under prevailing conditions, the realm of the social has "invaded" and "conquered" every domain of our activity (*OR* 233). As a consequence of the atomization and routinization of the social realm, we have increasingly come to "behave" rather than "act" and to "conform" rather than "excel."[16]

With the rise of the social, our political lives have been emptied of their potential for excellence and valor. In contrast, "excellence itself, *aretē* as the Greeks, *virtú* as the Romans would have called it" had "always been assigned to the public realm where one could excel, could distinguish oneself from all others." In this way, Arendt argues, the ancients could attain "an excellence never matched in privacy" (*HC* 48). Yet "our capacity for [such] action and speech has lost much of its former quality since the rise of the social realm banished these into the sphere of the intimate and the private" (*HC* 49). Depicting the implications of "the rise of the social" in the *Origins of Totalitarianism*, she again points to such factors as isolation, "massification," and the loss of civic spirit as the immediate preconditions for the emergence of totalitarian "movement-regimes."[17]

With her emphasis on the loss of the political tradition in the modern age, Arendt may appear to adopt Rousseau's view of "the political." But Arendt never subscribed to this view. Indeed, she was deeply disturbed by Rousseau's political thought. For the most part, her criticisms of Rousseau stem from the centrality he gives to the "sovereign will" in his civic community.[18] She reminds us that the universal law in Rousseau's state emanates from the purity of each person's own subjective will, without the need for discussion or communication with others. Given both her animosity toward subjectivity and the importance she attached to audience and speech in the "free" performance of political action, it is no doubt understandable why Arendt objects to the despotic implications of Rousseau's idea of the sovereign will. In her words,

> A state in which there is no communication between the citizens and where each man thinks only his own thoughts is by definition a tyranny. That the faculty of will and will-power in and by itself, unconnected with any other faculties, is an essentially nonpolitical and even anti-political capacity is perhaps nowhere else so manifest as in the absurdities to which Rousseau was driven and in the curious cheerfulness with which he accepted them. (*PF* 165)

Rather than gathering together a community of individuals who seek to live in accord with the pure dictates of their subjective will, says Arendt, politics is important as the collaboration and public discourse of equals working and speaking under the common aegis of a constitution. For her, the very idea of such collaboration and communication already assumes the existence of divisions and disagreement among citizens. Having equal status, they nevertheless hold different political recommendations and views. Against Rousseau's conception of citizenship, Arendt claims that the collective dimension of politics secures human dignity by demonstrating that citizens are not simply determined by the dictates of their inner will, but freely act and communicate with others in the luminescence of the public world. Through such acts and speech, citizens learn to shape and define their common destiny. Only in this way, she argues, can the domain of human freedom be protected from "the pernicious and dangerous consequences" of Rousseau's theory (*PF* 164).

Arendt is undoubtedly critical of the "pretext of tyranny" Rousseau's theory of the sovereign will provides, yet her own theory nevertheless valorizes freedom in its ancient form. For this reason, some have argued that Arendt ironically opens herself up to the same objections that Constant raised against Rousseau. Recall Constant's sociological claim that ethical ideas and political choices are constrained by the historical development of social conditions and institutions within which these ideas and choices are to be enforced.

On the basis of this claim, it could be said that Arendt elaborates an idea of freedom that cannot be supported under present conditions.

For instance, it is often noted that Arendt all but neglects the importance of representative institutions in the U.S. polity.[19] For her, it is said, such representation may bring some good about, but in principle, it cannot establish a system of legitimate political freedom. Only the direct participation of the citizenry can do that. But for many of her liberal-minded critics, such neglect cannot be justified on this basis. Rather, like Constant, they see representation not only as the most appropriate system of government for establishing and protecting modern individual liberty but as an essential ingredient of individual liberty itself. Hence, by criticizing individual liberty and largely dismissing the value of representation, it is said, Arendt's theory poses ethical demands that simply cannot be institutionally enforced.

Moreover, not unlike Rousseau, Arendt has been charged with so-called dangerous anachronism. This criticism can again be understood in terms of Constant's sociological theory. Recall that for Constant, the ethical standards of one historical age are often dangerous when applied to prevailing institutional conditions. Drawing from this principle, Stephen Holmes has argued that, "by linking totalitarianism so closely with 'the loss of the political,' Arendt neglects the plausibility of Constant's thesis that the most appalling form of modern tyranny may actually contain a distorted echo of ancient freedom."[20] In Holmes's opinion, "she could have corrected this blind spot if she had replaced her simplistic theory of the "rise of the social" with a theory more adequate to the increased structural differentiation of modern society" (117).

But such claims against Arendt need not go unanswered. First, it should be noted that the force of her analysis is based neither on her desire to, nor on her belief in, the possibility of returning to the halcyon days of the Greeks or Romans. Rather, her theory is dedicated to both therapeutic and edifying goals: She recollects, revivifies, and revitalizes the metaphors and ideals of the past in order to demonstrate what has been lost in the present. Recalling the memory of the past, she attempts to overcome the delusions of our belief that by securing individual liberty and constructing a system of representation we can attain self-governance and democratic freedom.

In making this point, Arendt challenges the very coherence of our notion of representation. Understood either as a fiduciary role (representing the trust of one's constituents) or as a reflective role (representing the expressed concerns and interests of one's constituents), the very idea of re-presenting a citizen misses the point of Aristotle's claim that politics is an inherently valuable activity. For Aristotle, presenting oneself in public is an important part of the development of our character and virtue. It changes the kind of persons we are. In Arendt's terms, if one considers that the "self" that is being re-presented is shaped through public self-presentation, then the idea of "representation" itself appears incoherent. How can anyone else re-present us? For Arendt, this question is not meant to imply that representation cannot serve a useful function in modern government. Rather, her point is that representation cannot replace the idea of political freedom defined as the direct participation (public self-presentation) of citizens in determining their collective destiny.

Of course, no matter how much we might admire it, her depiction of the Aristotelian citizen appears fairly remote to prevailing conditions and practices. But, again, the claim that her conception amounts to little more than empty nostalgia misses the point of her argument. For Arendt, by sociologically circumscribing our prevailing practices, we tend to reify the present and endorse the status quo. In contrast, her mission is one of edification, not reification. Precisely because her vision is remote, it challenges our current practices. Cast against the failures of the present, it gives voice to radical impulses of emancipation. In urging us to transform our institutions and self-conceptions, she thus acts to expand our cultural and political imaginations. In this respect, there may be a danger to the status quo in Arendt's theory, but it does not follow that her theory thereby offers a pretext for modern tyranny. Unless one assumes that any threat to the status quo is *ex hypothesi* tyrannical, one simply cannot link theoretical anachronism to political tyranny without a good deal more argument.

As we have seen, such an argument generally takes two forms in Constant's work. First, he criticized the notion of the universal will ascribed to Rousseau's theory of political freedom. Expressed in the acts of Napoleon and the Revolutionary Terror, such a conception poses an obvious danger to modern politics. Second, he criticized Rousseau's neglect of the importance of individual liberty in modern regimes. According to Constant, without such liberty, the individual remains vulnerable to, and is left unprotected against, the overwhelming authority and power of the state.

Unlike Constant, Arendt does not appear to advocate either the universality attributed to Rousseau's concept of freedom or the complete denial of the role of individual liberty. In regard to the former, we have already witnessed Arendt's criticism of the concept of the universal that is forged from the collective subjectivity of Rousseau's citizens. In regard to the latter, Arendt sharply distinguishes individual liberty from political freedom precisely because we tend to conflate the two. By valorizing the latter over the former, she need not be seen as rejecting the claims for individual liberty. Rather, her point is that individual liberty can be dangerous to a polity if it is not accompanied by public discussion, debate, and participation. Indeed, in her view, political freedom provides the best defense against the rise of modern totalitarian regimes.

Even if Arendt could be acquitted of the charges of dangerous anachronism and the neglect of representation, there is nevertheless an element of her theory that paradoxically seems to challenge her own views. By completely divorcing the private and social, on the one hand, from the political, on the other, Arendt appears to empty the substantive content of her own ideal.[21] Rather than bounding these spheres off against each other in order to distinguish their proper roles, Arendt severs all links between these realms. For her, the concerns of the social have monopolized political discourse. In order to overcome this monopolization, she banishes the social from the domain of the political. "To be bounded off," however, implies that there must be links between these realms. By seeing the social as consumed by "mere economic issues" that ought not to contaminate the purity of politics, she tends to eliminate from "the political" concerns even Aristotle found central to public life. In particular, she banishes substantive discussions of (distributive) justice from public and political debate. Captured in its purity, her depiction of the revivification of the political is thus emptied of its content.

Richard Rorty's Romance of the Future

In contrast to Arendt's romance of the past, Rorty's is a romance of the future following Dewey. Although on occasion he has called himself a "tragic liberal," Rorty has nevertheless consistently endorsed utopian enterprises aimed at expanding one's political imagination through romantic visions of future greatness. "To imagine great things is to imagine a great future for a particular community, a community one knows well, identifies with, can make plausible predictions about. In the modern world, this usually means one's nation. Political romance is, therefore, for the foreseeable future, going to consist of psalms of national future, rather than of the future of mankind."[22] This idea may seem to substantiate the not uncommon claim made against Rorty's supposed ethnocentricity, but it should be noted that in his remarks, he is referring to the national future of Brazil, not the United States.[23]

However, in his most recent book, *Contingency, Irony and Solidarity*, Rorty may be closer to offering just such an American romance, one that dissolves or evades (rather than appropriates) the problems of the past by cashing in on the liberal hopes of the future. His psalm to the future takes the shape of a liberal utopia that ironically stresses its own historical contingency. Indeed, Rorty uses the term *ironist* "to name the sort of person who faces up to the contingency of his or her own most central beliefs and desires. . . . Liberal ironists are people who include among these ungroundable desires their own hope that suffering will be diminished, that the humiliation of human beings by other human beings may cease" (*CIS* xv). For Rorty, neither the romantic dreams of communitarian politics nor the equally empty hopes of metaphysicians can offer a foundation or grounding for human solidarity.[24] Rather, it is by becoming more sensitive to the often subtle forms of human cruelty that we expand and experience such solidarity. For instance, literary works like those by Vladimir Nabokov and George Orwell often warn us against the insidious "tendencies to cruelty inherent in searches for autonomy" (*CIS* 144).

By autonomy, Rorty means the kind of thing self-creating ironists like Nietzsche, Sartre, or Foucault seek (*CIS* 65). Like Derrida, he claims, in their search to destroy the transparency of linguistic exchange that Hegelian comedy attempted to establish, these thinkers tend to merely repeat what they endlessly deny. Unlike Derrida, however, Rorty believes that pragmatism provides a way of unravelling this tangle of endless repetition.

In Rorty's view, we should drop the idea that language speaks to us in an endlessly rupturing dialogue with the Other. Indeed, if one takes the pragmatic turn in language with Rorty, the "silent" voice of the ineffable Other might sound a bit like Wittgenstein's famous "unsayable." When we come upon that which is unsayable, Wittgenstein tells us, we are inclined to utter an inarticulate grunt. In Rorty's view, the ineffable Other may provoke a similar response. Of course, like Wittgenstein's, Rorty's point is that when we confront the unnameable proclaiming itself, we should not feel particularly obliged to find the linguistic experience either profane or sacred. Rather, it might be more useful to follow Rorty's pragmatic lead and ask such questions as: How did we get into this predicament in the first place? How could we linguistically find ourselves face-to-face with the ineffable Other? And, finding ourselves trapped inside this language game, how can we improvise to get out?

Further, if, like Rorty, one does not put much faith in the language of "presence," "representation," and "transparency," then one need not feel particularly threatened by the disruption of linguistic exchange that is said to rupture the foundation of language itself. Indeed, if one accepts the contingency of language, as Rorty clearly does, then one can simply drop the idea that language is foundational. Again in opposing such foundationalism, Rorty draws from Wittgenstein's metaphor of vocabularies as alternate tools that human beings use. Dropping the linguistic picture that holds us captive to the cycles of death and resurrection repeated in postmodern writers, Rorty urges us to use these tools to construct a better future.

While obviously critical of their "project," Rorty does not simply dismiss the works of such thinkers as Sartre, Foucault, and Nietzsche. Indeed, rather than either ignoring or politicizing their attempts at radical self-creation or self-perfection, he advocates privatizing their project of autonomy. "Privatize the Nietzschean-Sartrean-Foucauldian attempt at authenticity and purity," he tells us, "in order to prevent yourself from slipping into a political attitude which will lead you to think that there is some social goal more important than avoiding cruelty" (*CIS* 65).

Like Arendt, Rorty often employs the language of the "private" and the "public" to articulate his political thought. In contrast to Arendt, however, Rorty inverts the valence attached to these spheres. Publicly and politically, he endorses the institutions of contemporary liberal society that attempt to balance the preservation of individual liberty with the prevention of human suffering. In what must be read with a good deal of irony, Rorty tells us, "my hunch is that Western social and political thought may have had the *last* conceptual revolution it needs. J. S. Mill's suggestion that governments devote themselves to optimizing the balance between leaving people's private lives alone and preventing suffering seems to me pretty much the *last word*" (*CIS* 63). Indeed, as "*humanity's* most precious achievement," Rorty exclaims, "*nothing* is more important" than protecting "these liberal institutions" against "thugs and theorists" alike.[25]

Although there is much to be said on behalf of his liberal ideal, Rorty's "romance" appears to confirm a number of Arendt's deepest suspicions about the loss of political discourse and the rise of privatization. For its part, Arendt's quest for the recovery of the political seems to confirm Rorty's suspicions of those who celebrate a world that can no longer speak to our concerns; a world, he describes, as "well lost." In clarifying these positions, let me begin with a suspicion of my own.

To tell you the truth, I'm not sure whether Rorty's arguments about essentialism and anti-essentialism make any difference or all of the difference. Consider William James's definition of pragmatic truth: "The true is the name of whatever proves itself to be good in the way of belief, and good, too, for definite, assignable reasons."[26] While Rorty uses this definition as a tool for liberating us from the prison house of metaphysical language, a distinction between texts one thinks are good in the way of belief and those which one thinks are not good in the way of belief has nothing to do with whether or not such texts are "metaphysical" or "essentialist."

Rather, as James's definition indicates, the issue of whether or not a text or argument is "true" is a matter of life's practical struggles. For James, pragmatism serves as a mediator or reconciler; it "unstiffens" our theories and allows for a proliferation of thought on the concrete, practical matters of life (156). If a text, written in metaphysical language, provides principles or ideas that can be justified for us practically, then those principles should be held as valid, as true. In this respect, the truth of a theory simply does not hinge on whether it is written in essentialist or anti-essentialist language.

For Rorty, calling a work "metaphysical" or "essentialist" thus seems to be something of an empty insult. If one thinks that a narrative couched in "metaphysical" terms is "true" (in the Jamesian sense), then one can just strip it of its metaphysical language through redescription. If one does not believe such a narrative is "true," then one can call it "metaphysical" and essentially drop it.

To cite an obvious example, even though John Stuart Mill has the last word in his romance, Rorty's utopian politics are nevertheless drawn from the *bête noire* of modern antimetaphysical thinking, Immanuel Kant. Just as John Rawls has shed Kant's metaphysical trappings by canceling the "idea of a transhistorical" and "absolutely valid" set of concepts that would serve as "philosophical foundations" of liberalism, Rorty identifies his own pragmatic romance with the "self-fulfilling triumph of the Enlightenment" (*CIS* 57).

Indeed, from Rorty's narrative perspective, a nonmetaphysical, nonfoundational, self-canceling, and contingent reading of Kant's *Metaphysical Elements of Justice* would almost certainly amount to a pragmatic redescription of Rawls' first principle. Recall Kant's "Universal Principle of Justice": "I ought to act in such a way that my freedom can co-exist with the freedom of every other." Although justifying this claim for freedom in terms of our historically contingent beliefs, both Rawls and Rorty undoubtedly endorse the fulfillment of Kant's liberal project. Moreover, by de-scientizing and de-philosophizing his enlightened thought, Rorty makes Kant's liberalism converge with that of Jefferson, whom Rorty also depicts as a first rate liberal thinker with some bad metaphysical habits (PD 257-258). With their metaphysical remnants of Enlightenment rationalism stripped away, however, both Jefferson and Kant can finally be included in the ranks of such good liberals as Isaiah Berlin and J. S. Mill, not to mention Benjamin Constant. In this way, if Kant led philosophy departments astray for the last two hundred years, it seems that Rorty has not strayed too far from an updated, American version of Kant's utopian ideal of liberalism.

In his American romance, Rorty employs metaphors that are undoubtedly part of our dominant cultural vocabulary. For instance, he tells us that the U.S. tradition of pragmatic thought allows us to "cash in" on our ideas. Rather than advocating "wholesale" constraints on conversation, Rorty appeals to what he calls "the retail reasons which have brought one to one's present view" (*CP* 165). In this way, as Christopher Norris has pointed out, in language "akin to current economists' parlance," Rorty uses the word liberal to describe "a kind of intellectual free-market outlook which wants to have done with all restrictive or legitimating checks and controls."[27]

Paradoxically, though he employs its dominant metaphor, Rorty pays little or no attention to economic analysis in constructing his liberal utopia. Indeed, it is not clear whether economic issues themselves are to be considered "private" or "public" in Rorty's view. In this respect, the very distinction Rorty uses to articulate his liberal romance tends to be fairly useless in examining the very domain from which his metaphorical exchange is derived. Here, somewhat as in Arendt, the problem lies in Rorty's use of a distinction that simply cannot account for the way in which a plurality of spheres are both "linked together" and "bound off against each other" in a complex culture. For this reason, Rorty's wholesale use of the private and the public to articulate his political vision is as inappropriate as his wholesale distribution and monopolization of the metaphor of exchange.

Of course, the implication of Rorty's proliferation of the metaphor of exchange goes well beyond the problem it might pose for his understanding of the marketplace. Recall that as a strong poet, Rorty gives an account of intellectual history and philosophy that follows Nietzsche's definition of "truth" as "a mobile army of metaphors" (*CIS* 17). Intellectual history may be conceived, he argues, as the nonteleological evolution of metaphoric redescriptions. In his words, "Old metaphors are constantly dying off into literalness, and then serving as a platform and foil for new metaphors" (*CIS* 16). The strong poets of history are those persons who develop new vocabularies as tools "for doing things which could not even have been envisaged before these tools were available" (*CIS* 17).

Rorty's metaphoric vision of intellectual evolution reflects some of the characteristics that Alexis de Tocqueville first associated with American philosophy: "To treat tradition as valuable for information only and to accept existing facts as no more than a useful sketch to show how things could be done differently and better—such are the principal characteristics of American philosophy" (*DA* 429). Unlike either Arendt's vision of the loss of U.S. political freedom or Allan Bloom's *Closing of the American Mind*, Rorty's works criticize romances that yearn for "a world well lost" (*CP* 3f.).[28] In contrast, as we have just seen, Rorty views the past itself as a series of ossified metaphors that provide the platform for developing alternate vocabularies that "show how things could be done differently and better" (*DA* 429).

Concentrating on these old metaphors, Rorty often wages his attack on the "metaphysical" commitments of the past. But he can successfully dismiss these "metaphysical" ideas only by taking their metaphorical structure literally. This point might best be expressed in terms of an analogy. It is often said that every good comedian needs a straight man. The reason for this is that for comedy to have its ironic effect, it needs to play off the literal. In a similar respect, Rorty seems to have found a number of straight men in the history of philosophy. In order for his irony to work, he must understand them as if they were actually offering a description of the way the world really is. By showing that their descriptions are really metaphors that have become literalized, Rorty paradoxically criticizes the metaphors of the past as if they were *really* literal.

In contrast, Arendt attempts to reawaken these old metaphors. As a therapeutic measure, she uses the past to challenge our present prejudices. As an edifying movement, she opens the horizons of our historical imagination "in order to show how things could be done differently and better" (*DA* 429). By dismissing as merely ossified metaphor the kind of foundationalist language Arendt employs, Rorty's criticism of the Romantics of the past appears deeply misguided. Once again, as James reminds us, metaphysics or foundationalism is not at issue in pragmatic thought. What is at issue is whether a text offers us a better way of dealing with life's practical struggles.

Following James, if we drop the idea that it matters whether a narrative is "metaphysical," then, unlike Rorty, we can offer a reading of our cultural history that is more complex than one that tells of the triumph of "good" pragmatics over "bad" metaphysical ideas. To illustrate this point, consider for the final time the conflict of liberty and freedom. In defense of individual liberty, Rorty follows Berlin in arguing against all telic conceptions of freedom, notions defined in terms of a determinate set of moral ends (*CIS* 45). In Berlin's view, the freedom of political participation itself often falls under this rubric. Indeed, in approaching such a dangerous metaphysical idea, he warns: "To block before man every door but one, no matter how noble the prospect upon which it opens . . . is to sin against the truth that he is a man, a being with a life of his own."[29] Like Berlin, Rorty has persistently argued that only through individual liberty can human beings be protected from such "sinful" philosophical acts (or their pragmatic analogues).

Of course, Berlin tends to portray these two concepts as mutually exclusive or, at least, deeply incompatible. Indeed, the latter is conceived as the very opposite of "true" liberty insofar as it entails a telic or objective conception of human flourishing. But in the dispute between democratic freedom and individual liberty, there seems to be nothing linguistically, conceptually, or historically exclusive about these ideas. They simply do not live by each other's death.

For example, etymologically there may be elemental links between these principles in both Greek and Latin word families. As is widely held, the range of meanings of the Latin *liber*, the Greek *eleutheria*, the Venetic *leudheros*, and the Anglo-Saxon *freo* includes both "unobstructed movement" and "lawful self-government."[30] Historically, these two concepts have also often resided in concert with each other. For instance, Quentin Skinner has pointed out that even in Machiavelli's "republican" model of political freedom, "the negative idea of liberty as mere non-obstruction of individual agents in the pursuit of their chosen ends was combined with the ideas of virtue and public service" as moral or telic ends.[31]

And the principles of individual liberty and democratic freedom are frequently conceived as mutually reinforcing.[32] Consider, for example, Tocqueville's claim that the virtues of public participation not only play an important role in defending against the propensity toward individualism and atomization in the U.S. system but also play a paideutic role in teaching citizens to defend and protect their individual rights and liberties. In this way, a constitutional guarantee for individual liberty and an active participation in local affairs were conceived as a combined force of mutually supportive principles of the U.S. regime.

Nevertheless, to argue that there are etymological, historical, and conceptual links between these two principles means that they must be understood as distinct. And precisely because they are distinct, there are circumstances and conditions where they are bound to collide. Indeed, our respect for the differences between these principles makes such conflicts unavoidable. Both qualitatively and quantitatively, to be distinct means to be separated from by being bounded off against. Hence, zones of conflict often appear where boundaries meet—on the penumbra that bounds off and separates—distinct ethical principles and political traditions.

Part of a complex and pluralistic political culture, our differences often help to establish our identity. We often define ourselves in terms of the very disagreements and conflicts we confront as a people. In this respect, inherent in the etymological, historical, and conceptual links that bind us are the differences that separate us. In the zones of conflict that are bound to occur as a result of these differences, it is not surprising that we find what A. C. Bradley described as the "essential fact of tragedy."[33]

Yet by arguing so vehemently for individual liberty alone, Rorty ironically transforms one of the deepest conflicts within our political culture into yet another romantic presentation of good texts over bad texts, human sanctity over philosophical presumption, and freedom over enslavement. In this way, the irony, contingency, and solidarity of ethical life may require a greater respect for our conception of democratic freedom and public participation than can be found in Rorty's liberal romance.

And by arguing so vehemently for democratic freedom and public participation, Arendt appears as Rorty's mirrored double. In this respect, each displays the inverse image of the other's position. In the symmetry lying between the past and the future, the heroic warrior and the strong poet, the public and the private, the radical democrat and the enlightened liberal, each reflects what the other lacks. In Rorty, we see a vision of the future that lacks a vital past, a liberal utopia without public space. In Arendt, we find a vision of radical democracy cast against the "rise of the social," a Hellenic romance without ethical substance. As stories of triumph and possibility, of democratic freedom and individual liberty, they thus remain locked in a battle suspended.

The battle between those books written by Hannah Arendt and those authored by Richard Rorty constitutes the most recent eruption of the conflict of liberty and freedom. In this way, just as it was captured in the writings of Thomas Jefferson nearly two centuries ago, in contemporary debate there undoubtedly remains a vital tension between our desires for individual liberty, the value we place on moral plurality, and the demands of our political freedom. With this conflict intact, we end where we began. Like the episode between the gallant Basque and the valiant Quixote, we have returned to a battle suspended.

As a last, "supplemental" note, I'd like to tie up one of the threads I left dangling at the beginning of our discussion. Promising to search for an ending, Cervantes left chapter 8 and did not return for over six weeks. At the beginning of chapter 9, he recounts how he located the missing manuscript. He then returns to the story. The battle between the gallant Basque and the valiant Manchegan ends in much the way you would expect.

Notes

1. *The Federalist Papers*, ed. Isaac Kramnick (London: Penguin, 1987), 327.

2. In U.S. political thought, the terms of this debate are disputed. Rather than addressing contemporary arguments surrounding this dispute, I will focus on the definitions offered by Arendt and Rorty, respectively. On the terms of political discourse in dispute, see the definitions of liberalism, republicanism, democracy, and enlightenment proffered by Louis Hartz, *The Liberal Tradition in America* (New York: Harcourt Brace, 1955); J. G. A. Pocock, *The Machiavellian Moment: Florentine Political Thought and the Atlantic Republican Tradition* (Princeton, N.J.: Princeton University Press, 1975), ch. 15; Gordon S. Wood, *The Creation of the American Republic, 1776-1787* (Chapel Hill, N.C.: University of North Carolina Press, 1969); Wilson Carey McWilliams, *The Idea of Fraternity in America* (Berkeley and Los Angeles: University of California Press, 1973); Benjamin Barber, *Strong Democracy* (Berkeley and Los Angeles: University of California Press, 1984); Terence Ball, *Transforming Political Discourse* (Oxford: Blackwell, 1988), ch. 3; and Thomas Pangle, *The Spirit of Modern Republicanism* (Chicago: University of Chicago Press, 1988), esp. part I.

3. Richard Rorty, "The Priority of Democracy to Philosophy," in *The Virginia Statute for Religious Freedom: Its Evolution and Consequences*, ed. Merrill D. Peterson and Robert C. Vaughan (Cambridge: Cambridge University Press, 1988), 257-282.

4. Hannah Arendt, *On Revolution* (New York: Viking, 1963). Cited below as *OR*. See Jefferson's 1816 letters to Joseph C. Cabell and Samuel Kercheval in *Jefferson Writings*, ed. Merrill D. Peterson (New York: Library of America, 1984).

5. Recall Hegel's description of the "cauldron of sentimentality" out of which the Romantic poets were said "to serve up their broth of heart, friendship, and inspiration," in *Philosophy of Right*, trans. T. M. Knox (Oxford: Oxford University Press, 1942), 6.

6. See Arendt's discussion of "World Alienation," in *The Human Condition* (Chicago: University of Chicago Press, 1958), 248-257. Cited below as *HC*.

7. Tolstoy's remark is repeated in Max Weber's famous essay "Vom Inneren Beruf zur Wissenschaft." See *Max Weber: Soziologie, Weltgeschichtliche Analysen, Politik*, ed. Johannes Winckelmann (Stuttgart: Alfred Kröner, 1964), 317.

8. Arendt is not always clear on the relation between the private and the social. She frequently describes the social as the modern analogue to the private. Yet she also distinguishes these realms by suggesting that the social is neither fully private nor public ("The Rise of the Social," in *HC* 38f.). See discussion below.

9. See book 1 of Aristotle's *Politics* for a similar division of function. See also my discussion in Chapter 1.

10. A number of authors have pointed out the masculine quality of Arendt's depiction of politics. See, for example, Hanna Pitkin's criticism in "On Relating Private and Public," *Political Theory* 9 (August 1981): 331-338.

11. Richard Rorty, *Contingency, Irony and Solidarity* (Cambridge: Cambridge University Press, 1989), 53. Cited below as *CIS*.

12. Richard Rorty, *Consequence of Pragmatism* (Minneapolis, Minn.: University of Minnesota Press, 1982), 153. Cited below as *CP*.

13. Hannah Arendt, "On Violence," in *Crisis of the Republic* (New York: Harcourt Brace Jovanovich, 1972), 114; cited below as OV.

14. Much like Hegel's, Arendt's fear of the destructive force of liberation is expressed in her views on the Revolutionary Terror of 1791. See *OR*, 74-75.

15. Alexis de Tocqueville, *Democracy in America*, trans. George Lawrence, ed. J. P. Mayer (New York: Doubleday Anchor, 1969), 692. Cited below as *DA*.

16. In the French tradition, Pierre Royer-Collard and Tocqueville first analyzed the paradox that with increased social atomization, individualism tended to strengthen social conformity

17. See Hannah Arendt, *On the Origins of Totalitarianism* (New York: World Press, 1958), 305-326.

18. See Hannah Arendt, "What is Freedom?" in *Between Past and Future* (New York: Viking Press, 1968). Cited below as *PF*. Arendt's criticism of the sovereign will is not unlike the criticism Hegel leveled against both Rousseau and Kant's abstract notion of the inner will as that which dictates universal

moral law. For example, see his remarks on absolute freedom and pietism in the *Phenomenology of Spirit*, trans. A. V. Miller (Oxford: Oxford University Press, 1981).

19. For example, see George Kateb, *Hannah Arendt: Politics, Conscience, Evil* (Oxford: Martin Robertson, 1983), 23-24.

20. Stephen Holmes, "Aristippus in and out of Athens," *American Political Science Review* 73 (March 1979): 117.

21. From a different approach, Pitkin makes much the same argument in "Private and Public," 348-349.

22. Richard Rorty, "Unger, Castoriadis, and the Romance of a National Future," *Northwestern University Law Review* 82 (Winter 1988): 343.

23. For such a criticism see Mark C. Taylor, "Paralectics," in *Tears* (Albany: State of New York Press, 1990), 123-144.

24. See Rorty's critical remarks on communitarianism in "The Priority of Democracy." See also his criticism of Charles Taylor, *CP* 200-202, and his discussion of the "Contingency of Community," *CIS* 23-44.

25. Richard Rorty, "Thugs and Theorists," *Political Theory* 15 (November 1987): 567.

26. William James, *Essays on Pragmatism*, ed. Alburey Castell (New York: Hafner, 1951), 155.

27. Christopher Norris, *Contest of Faculties* (London: Methuen, 1985), 153.

28. See also Richard Rorty's review of Allan Bloom's *Closing of the American Mind* (New York: Simon and Shuster, 1987) in "That Old Time Philosophy," *New Republic* 198 (April 1988): 28-33.

29. Isaiah Berlin, "Two Concepts of Liberty," in *Four Essays on Liberty* (New York: Oxford University Press, 1969), 126.

30. See Hanna Pitkin, "Are Freedom and Liberty Twins?" *Political Theory* 16 (November 1988): 529.

31. Quentin Skinner, "The Idea of Negative Liberty," in *Philosophy in History*, ed. Richard Rorty, Jerome B. Schneewind and Quentin Skinner (Cambridge: Cambridge University Press, 1984), 197.

32. See L. A. Seidentop, "Two Liberal Traditions," in *The Idea of Freedom*, ed. Alan Ryan (Oxford: Oxford University Press, 1979), 153-174. See also Richard Flathman's concluding arguments in *The Philosophy and Politics of Freedom* (Chicago: University of Chicago Press, 1987), 303-322.

33. A. C. Bradley, *Oxford Lectures on Poetry* (Oxford: Oxford University Press, 1950), 70.

PART THREE

Conclusion

7

Putting the "E" Back into *Différance*

A term almost as fashionable as irony these days is the Other. One hears about all sorts of Others in discursive currency. There is Sartre's Other as an imago of hell; there is the mystical Other as that which we cannot grasp or comprehend; there is the Other involved in every dialectical formulation; there is the anthropological Other that stands in opposition to us as a reflection of ourselves; and there are other Others that are variously said to speak us, confront us, or define us.

In this concluding chapter, I want to offer a first step in clarifying a portion of the semantic field of the Other by examining three kinds of otherness: The Other as dialectic, the Other as ineffable, and the Other as different. The first is best exemplified in the work of G.W.F. Hegel; the second is familiar to those, like Derrida, who write on the unspeakable silence of *différance*; and the third probably finds its source in Aristotle but is relatively neglected in contemporary Continental debate.[1] As a way of distinguishing between these three Others, I trace the divergent readings of Sophocles' *Antigone* that can be adduced when the central conflict of the play is viewed as a struggle among the "dialectical," the "ineffable" and the "different." After assessing the strengths and limits of these views, I end by suggesting that we put the "e" back into *différance*. In other words, I claim that we need to learn to do justice to the Other, as neither dialectical nor ineffable, but as different.

The Dialectics of Comedy

While Hegel's articulation of the structure of the modern state may represent the final realization of objective spirit in the world, it is certainly not the end of the story of the odyssey of *Geist*. Indeed, in its objective moment, Hegel claimed, *Geist* is grasped only one-sidedly. It is grasped only in terms of a particular state set within particular temporal and spatial dimensions. Hence, though it may well reveal the principle of the state in its totality, it does not reveal this principle in its universal form:

> At a higher level, the life of the state, as a whole, does form a perfect totality in itself: . . . but the principle itself . . . is still once again one-sided and inherently abstract. . . . It is only the rational freedom of the will which is explicit here; it is only in the state and once again only this individual state—and therefore again in a particular sphere of existence . . . that freedom is actual. Thus man feels too that the rights and obligations in these regions and their mundane and, once more, finite mode of existence are insufficient; he feels that both in their objective character, and also in their relation to the subject, they need a still higher confirmation and sanction.[2]

This higher confirmation, he tells us, can only be found in the region of Absolute truth. It is within this region that we find the highest form of Hegel's "divine" comedy, where essential harmony is established and all contradiction resolved: "The highest truth, truth as such, is the resolution of the highest opposition and contradiction. In its validity and power, the opposition between freedom and necessity, between spirit and nature, between knowledge and its object, between law and impulse, indeed opposition and contradiction as such, whatever forms they may take are swept away" (*LA* I.100).

As the sensuous expression of the Absolute, art is the first stop on Hegel's journey to this higher realm of resolution. Setting "truth before our minds in the mode of sensuous configuration," Hegel tells us, art itself reaches its highest expression in Sophocles' *Antigone*. As a philosopher and teacher, Hegel could not claim modesty as one of his primary virtues. In his *Lectures on Fine Arts*, he tells us: "Of all the masterpieces of the classical and the modern world—and I know nearly all of them, and you should and can—the *Antigone* seems to me to be the most magnificent and satisfying work of art" (*LA* II.1216). For Hegel, the *Antigone* exemplified the development of tragic conflict in its purest dialectical form (*LA* II.1217). In this work, he claimed: "Family piety is expounded . . . as principally the law of woman. . . . This law is there displayed as a law opposed to public law, to the law of the land. This is the supreme opposition in ethics and therefore in tragedy; and it is individualized in the same play in the opposing natures of man and woman" (*PR* 166).

Although Hegel's dialectical reading of the *Antigone* continues to have strong contemporary support, many have justifiably questioned the essentialism underlying Hegel's characterization of gender differentiation. For him, man and woman are, by nature, different in respect to their capacities for excellence. In a well-known addition to the *Philosophy of Right*, Hegel makes his position all too clear:

> The difference between men and women is like that between animals and plants. Men correspond to animals, while women correspond to plants because their development is more placid and the principle that underlies it is the rather vague unity of feeling. When women hold the helm of government, the state is at once in jeopardy, because women regulate their actions not by the demands of universality but by arbitrary inclinations and opinions. (166A)

In addition to rejecting this kind of essentialism, many have also questioned the hierarchical strategy Hegel employed in overcoming the "supreme opposition" depicted in Sophocles' play.[3] Just as man is hierarchically placed over woman, so the ethical requirements of the political state are privileged over the values associated with kinship ties. There are good grounds for criticizing this hierarchical view. Yet, as Martha Nussbaum suggests, the very idea of dialectically overcoming this opposition may be problematic:

> To do justice to the nature or identity of two distinct values, requires doing justice to their difference; and doing justice to their difference—both their qualitative distinctness and their numerical separateness—requires seeing that there are, at least potentially, circumstances in which the two will collide. Distinctness requires articulation from, bounding-off against. This, in turn, entails the possibility of opposition—and for the agent who is committed to both—of conflict.[4]

To follow Nussbaum, it seems that though the moral requirements and principles of a political culture may be different, there is no reason to believe that they are dialectically related. Indeed, conflict seems unavoidable in a culture precisely because the values in opposition are distinct, not dialectical. Often appropriate to different semantic fields and spheres of ethical activity, they neither yearn for nor yield to the Other as dialectical. Rather, they oppose each other as a result of being bounded off against one another. Hegel's reading notwithstanding, such appears to be the case in the *Antigone*.

Creon and Antigone are not emblematic of dialectical opposition. They are instead emblematic of the different discursive and ethical practices contained within their cultural community. Although offering different descriptions of their practices and embracing different principles and beliefs, they do not necessarily manifest an internal logic of sublation. In other words, there may be no identifiable ethical idea in virtue of which they gain their unity. Creon and Antigone express not the self-division and intestinal warfare of the ethical substance, but the fragile contours and boundaries of the ethical landscape of a people.

By depicting tragedy as an instance of spiritual self-division, however, Hegel redescribes the narrative landscape of ethical life. He redraws the contours of *Sittlichkeit*, aligning them with the internal demands of his logic of sublation. Rather than seeing political culture as a complex association of differences that are apt to collide, he sees tragic conflicts as dialectically linked oppositions to be overcome. This is the fundamental difference between "difference" and "dialectical otherness."

The Ineffable Other

Recently, deconstructionists have focused on the political implications arising from the problems of difference and otherness. Consider, for example, how Mark Taylor opens what he calls the "Encore" to his work *Altarity*:

> The history of society and culture is, in large measure, a history of the struggle with the endlessly complex problems of difference and otherness. Never have the questions posed by difference and otherness been more pressing than they are today. For an era dominated by the struggle between among, and against various "isms"—communism, fascism, totalitarianism, capitalism, racism, sexism, etc.—the issue of difference is undeniably political. Is difference tolerable? Are others to be encouraged to express and cultivate their differences? Or is difference intolerable? Are others who are different to be converted, integrated, dominated, excluded, or repressed?[5]

No doubt, Taylor is quite right in suggesting the "undeniably political" urgency of the issue of difference. To offer an example apposite to the *Antigone*, the voices of women have too often been silenced, submerged, and forced to enter what Taylor might call the realm of the Other, the region silently stretching beyond the circumference of "normal" discursive practice and acknowledged ethical meaning. In general, this systematic exclusion results in a politics of appropriation and domination.

But, there is a difference between the "other as different" and Taylor's "ineffable other." To distinguish between these positions, it is important to begin by reemphasizing the parasitic relation between the "ineffable" and Hegel's "dialectical" Other. For Taylor, as for many postmoderns, the former "is neither positive nor negative, neither is nor is not." As the "ineffable and unspeakable," it is an Other that "cannot be dialectically sublated through the duplicitous positivity of double negation."[6] In this respect, the Other satirizes Hegel's idea of sublation by simultaneously creating the space for dialogue and neutralizing the transparency of the signs exchanged.[7] In other words, Hegel's system appears to be predicated on that which it systematically excludes: the ineffable Other. Speaking the unsayable, deconstructionists thus engage in a satirical dialogue that constantly disrupts, interrupts, and ruptures itself at every pause.

No one has offered better examples of such satirical dialogues than Derrida. In satirizing and disrupting Hegel's comic vision, Derrida explicitly focuses on the sexual politics of Hegel's reading of the *Antigone*. For Derrida, femininity is both suppressed by the dominant voice of Hegel's rationality and, at the same time, radically subverts the dominant (metaphysical) mode of his male (phallocentric) discourse.[8] In *Glas*, he at once embraces and deconstructs Hegel's claim that femininity is the "internal enemy" of political community.[9] Like that of deconstruction itself, woman's weapon of subversion is irony.

To exemplify the intimate bonds between deconstruction and "femininity," consider Derrida's ironic inversion of Hegel's claim that women are not subject to the self-division and inner diremption required to gain entry into civil society and human law. In their singularity, immediacy, and unity, Hegel tells us, they are substantively identified with the desires and feelings of the family and private law. In Other, deconstructive terms, Derrida writes: "Human law, the law of the rational community that institutes itself against the private law of the family, always suppresses femininity, stands up against it, girds, squeezes, curbs, compresses it" (187). Born by Hegel's desire to relieve (sublate) the conflict between the family and civil society, man must overcome (suppress, devour, engulf) the family itself. But, Derrida warns, "let one not go and see" in this precipitant "overcoming," "the end of phallocentrism, of idealism, of metaphysics" (188).

Rather, in his idea of sublation we find the limit of masculine power, a limit met by "the all-powerful weapon" of woman, *irony* (187). As "the everlasting irony of the community," woman "changes by intrigue the universal end of the government into a possession and ornament for the family" (187). Subverting Hegel's thesis, woman thus "turns to ridicule the earnest wisdom of mature age which, dead to pleasure and enjoyment only thinks of and cares for the universal" (188). Against this radically subversive element, Hegel's community must redouble its efforts to suppress the feminine (188).

But this dynamic of suppression only produces the irony of femininity it suppresses as its own "essential moment" (188). In this way woman "indefinitely harasses, questions, ridicules, mocks the essence, the truth (of man)" (188). In other words, suppression forever produces subversion in an endless play. Indeed, Derrida claims, they are mirrored doubles: Hegel's ruse of reason is just the other side of woman's eternal irony. In Derrida's words, rational cunning and feminine irony are "each able to take itself for the other and *to play the other*" (188). For this reason, he concludes, "If God is (probably) a man in speculative dialectics, the godness of God—the irony that divides him and makes him come off his hinges—the infinite disquiet of his essence is (if possible) woman(ly)" (188).

As we have already seen, in "Les Fins de l'homme," Derrida explores the possibility of producing a kind of philosophy that does not entertain the logocentric and phallocentric dominance that culminated in Hegel's metaphysics of presence.[10] In criticizing this tradition, Derrida deploys his unspeakable notion of *différance*.[11]

For Derrida, *différance* is the fund from which any established terms of relation between identity and difference might become reconfigured. Yet such reconfiguration is impeded by the parasitism of his deconstruction, which prevents Derrida from escaping the language and structure of that which he subverts. In this sense, he tends to repeat or invert rather than reconfigure the differences contained within Sophocles' *Antigone*.

A Different Kind of Otherness

Against both Hegel's dialectical Other and Derrida's ineffable Other, I have already alluded to a different conception of the Other. As a way of further defining and assessing this conception, I will briefly trace how this third Other is bounded off from the other—ineffable and dialectical—Others. In particular, I will concentrate on the lessons that we learn from the way these three kinds of otherness approach the ethical conflict of *Antigone*.

The differences between Creon and Antigone may best be understood as differences in their respective "ways of life."[12] These differences are expressed in terms of the distinct moral principles and ethical requirements they hold in relation to the familial, political, and religious spheres of their cultural community. Each of the characters is authoritative because each represents recognizable patterns of thought and action contained within the complex political culture of Athens. Creon aligns with the principle of loyalty to one's political association. He stresses the human capacity for dominion and control over the world of nature. His gods are Olympian, but his conception of justice is anthropocentric. Antigone's loyalty, on the other hand, is oriented toward kinship ties. For her, human beings are part of the web of nature, not its master. Appealing to the principle of divine justice, she worships the old chthonic gods cast in eternal time.

Instead of duplicating Hegel's comic quest to overcome the conflict between Antigone and Creon through the dialectical sublation of the Other, we learn—from an understanding of the Other as different—that "there is no standing ground, no place for enquiry, no way to engage in the practices of advancing, evaluating, accepting, and rejecting a particular ethical view apart from that which is provided by some other—different—position."[13] Hence, it is not from a single standard or sublated view, but from our respective differences that we gain our critical perspective.

It is important to emphasize that respecting differences is not the same as tolerating, assimilating, or merely integrating diverse views. It is not based on benign acceptance nor predicated on our rights to differ in our ethical ideas (as long as they do not interfere with others). Nor is it based on absorbing our differences into an integrated whole. Rather, it requires an active engagement with the Other, a critical dialogue in which the significance of rival views is recognized and challenged while, at the same time, our own views are similarly acknowledged and tested.

To do justice to our differences, we must first learn to see our cultural topography as a complex, multifaceted conjunction and disjunction of different vocabularies, traditions, activities, and practices. We must then learn to challenge the monopolization of our culture by any single value, dominant vocabulary, or privileged philosophical position. Rather than disrupting, disturbing, and dissolving Hegel's idea of dialectical sublation, such a respect for difference urges us to seek an understanding of our distinct discursive and ethical practices.

Applying this lesson to the *Antigone*, consider the different semantic fields referred to when Creon and Antigone use the terms *philos* or *ekhthros*. In Antigone's dialogue with Ismene, for example, she refers to their dead brother by claiming: "For me, the doer, death is best. / Friend [*philos*] shall I lie with him, yes friend [*philos*] with friend."[14] Now consider Creon's speech that begins, "My friends, the very gods who shook the state with mighty surge have set it straight again." In this famous passage, he goes on to declare that "he who counts another greater friend [*philos*] than his own fatherland, / I put him nowhere. / Nor could I count the enemy of the land friend [*philos*] to myself."[15] Of course, who counts as a friend or enemy is determined by the webs of meaning, the ethical and discursive practices, employed by each of these characters respectively. As distinct, these different semantic fields are both articulated from and bounded off against each other.

For members of Nietzsche's carnival of critics, however, such boundaries are invariably dissolved. Emphasizing the radical indeterminacy of ethical life, borders appear only to be exposed as illusory. The therapeutic result of such exposure is liberation from the deadweight of hierarchy and history with which we have silenced the voice of the Other. By dissolving these ossified boundaries, by giving voice to the Other, new vistas are said to arise.

Yet, as parasitic, these stories tend to repeat the very claims for transparency and purity they seek to destroy or deny. Indeed, as Derrida himself knows, such parasitism is bound to a dialectic of identity and alterity from which it cannot escape. Giving voice to the Other simply reverses the poles so that the tainted becomes the pure and the pure becomes tainted. Conceiving gender relations as a dialectic of identity and alterity often simply inverts their valence. In this way, giving voice to the female Other has a tendency to create what might be called a male alterity. Where women were understood as both "outside" and "debased," now men take on that tainted disposition of alterity. Once again, the pure becomes tainted whereas the tainted becomes pure. The question is whether there is a way to escape this trap of repetition and denial, of identity and alterity? Is there a form of politics that avoids the problems inherent in this dialectical dance?

In my view, gender ought not to be at issue in doing justice to the differences between what Hegel called the "supreme opposition" in ethics. Both men and women have the capacity for excellence in the spheres of the family and the state. Both can partake in the different ways of life articulated and expressed in the characters of Creon and Antigone, respectively. To object to the gendered characterization of this conflict, however, is neither to accept the present arrangements (or meaning) of power nor to deny that domination has resulted from the exclusion of women from the domain of public life. Nor is this meant to imply that the West has refrained from hierarchically arranging these different spheres of activity and ways of life. Nor should we be satisfied with a simple and uncritical division between the public and the private. Rather, we must begin to critically analyze the differences between different publics—the public as state apparatus, as economic practice, or as local participatory and democratic spheres of activity. Similarly, we must begin to distinguish between different privates—the private as domestic or familial, as politically exclusionary, or as a protected sphere of personal conduct. And finally, we must critically examine the interrelation, tension, and conflict among these various spheres of our practice.

As Other, women must reject the suffocating effects produced by a discourse of domination. And just as we must reject the discursive practice which denies women the opportuntity to speak and define themselves, we must also refuse to accept a one-dimensional portrait of humankind: women as victims or seductresses, men as tyrants or cuckolds. Only in this way can we display the complexity of human experience without reducing it to a set of simplistic polarities. Men are no more immune to weakness than women and women possess no secret powers over men. To acknowledge one's emotions is not to lose one's identity, one's sexuality. To lock women and men into gender specified roles is to deny them their full humanity.[16]

Rather than either embracing the comic hopes of dialectical sublation or the endless play of identity and alterity, I would like to end by suggesting that we put the "e" back into *différance*. In other words, we need to think of differences that do not yearn for the Other as dialectically related, differences that are not parasitic upon the Other, differences that are both bounded off and linked together. Here we find the elemental difference between *différance* and difference. By putting the "e" back into *différance*, we preserve the plurality and complexity of our discursive and cultural practices. Like the "ineffable" Other, this third kind of otherness both resists and challenges the suppression and monopolization inherent in Hegel's idea of sublation. But unlike the "unspeakable proclaiming itself," a critical view of our differences does not commit us to the endless play of resurrecting the dead only to kill it (as in the case of Creon) or be killed by it (as in the case of Antigone). In Greek tragedy it is amazing how often the dead keep killing the living. "A terror raging back, back into the future," as Aeschylus put it.[17] Perhaps this, too, is the wisdom that Sophocles sought to teach us in depicting the central conflict of his play? Perhaps it is a lesson we still have to learn.

Notes

1. On the Aristotelian connection, see Martha Nussbaum, *Fragility of Goodness* (Cambridge: Cambridge University Press, 1986).

2. G.W.F. Hegel, *Lectures on Fine Arts*, trans. T. M. Knox (Oxford: Oxford University Press, 1975), I.99. Cited below as *LA*.

3. For example, see Simon Goldhill, *Reading Greek Tragedy* (Cambridge: Cambridge University Press, 1986), 88-90.

4. Nussbaum, *Fragility of Goodness*, 68.

5. Mark C. Taylor, *Altarity* (Chicago: University Press, 1987), xxi.

6. Mark C. Taylor, "Paralectics," in *Tears* (Albany, NY: State of New York Press, 1990), 140.

7. Ibid., 140.

8. Following a good deal of contemporary French feminist writing, Derrida uses "woman" to signify any radical force that subverts the concepts, assumptions, and structures of traditional male (phallocentric) discourse. This use of the "feminine Other" is evident not only in Derrida's reading of Hegel, but in his analyses of Nietzsche (in *Spurs*) and Rousseau (in the *Grammatology*) as well. On the deployment of the "feminine Other" in contemporary French feminist thought, see Jonathan Culler, *Theory and Criticism After Structuralism*, (Ithaca, N.Y.: Cornell University Press, 1982), 43-64, and *New French Feminisms*, ed. Elaine Marks and Isabelle de Courtivron (Amherst: University of Massachusetts Press, 1980).

9. Jacques Derrida, *Glas*, trans. John P. Leavey, Jr., and Richard Rand (Lincoln: University of Nebraska Press, 1990), 188.

10. Jacques Derrida, "Les Fins de l'homme," in *Marges de la philosophie* (Paris: Editions de Minuit, 1972), 129-164.

11. See "Différance" in *Marges de la philosophie* (Paris: Editions de Minuit, 1972), 1-31.

12. See Charles Segal's recapitulation of these different ways of life in "*Antigone*: Death and Love, Hades and Dionysus," in *Greek Tragedy: Modern Essays in Criticism*, ed. Erich Segal (New York: Harper and Row, 1983), 174f. On the concept of a "way of life" see Aaron Wildavsky, Michael Thompson, and Richard Ellis, *Cultural Theory* (Boulder, Colo.: Westview Press, 1990).

13. Here I am transforming a similar argument made in Alasdair MacIntyre's *Whose Justice? Which Rationality?* (Notre Dame, Ind.: University of Notre Dame Press, 1988), 350.

14. *Antigone*, in *Sophocles I*, trans. Elizabeth Wyckoff (Chicago: University of Chicago Press, 1954), lines 80-100.

15. *Antigone*, lines 162-182. For a detailed analysis of the use of *philos* and *ekhthros* in this play, see Simon Goldhill, *Reading Greek Tragedy* (Cambridge: Cambridge University Press, 1986), 89-94.

16. See Margaret Brabant and Michael Brint, "Identity and Difference in Christine de Pizan's *Cité des Dames*" in *The Political Theory of Christine de Pizan*, ed. Margaret Brabant (Boulder, Colo.: Westview Press, forthcoming).

17. Aeschylus, *Agamemnon*, ed. T. E. Page (Cambridge, Mass.: Leob Classical Library, 1926), line 154.

Selected Bibliography

Aeschylus. *Agamemnon, Libation-Bearers, Eumenides*. Loeb Classical Library. 1926.

Alighieri, Dante. *Dantis Alagherii Epistolae*. Edited by Paget Toynbee. Oxford: Clarendon Press, 1966.

———. *La divina commedia*. Edited by Umberto Bosco and Giovanni Reggio. 3 vols. Firenze: Le Monnier, 1979.

Arendt, Hannah. *Between Past and Future*. New York: Viking Press, 1968.

———. *Crisis of the Republic*. New York: Harcourt Brace Jovanovich, 1972.

———. *Human Condition*. Chicago: University of Chicago Press, 1958.

———. *On Revolution*. New York: Viking, 1963.

———. *On the Origins of Totalitarianism*. New York: World Press, 1958.

Aristotle. *Politics*. Loeb Classical Library. 1932.

Bakhtin, Mikhail. *Rabelais and His World*. Translated by Helene Iswolsky. Cambridge, Mass.: MIT Press, 1965.

Ball, Terence. *Transforming Political Discourse*. Oxford: Blackwell, 1988.

Barber, Benjamin. *The Death of Communal Liberty*. Princeton, N.J.: Princeton University Press, 1974.

———. *Strong Democracy*. Berkeley and Los Angeles: University of California Press, 1984.

Barber, Benjamin, and Forman, Janis. "Preface to *Narcisse*." *Political Theory* 6 (November 1978): 537-554.

Berlin, Isaiah. *Concepts and Categories*. Introduction by Bernard Williams. London: Penguin, 1981.

———. *Four Essays on Liberty*. New York: Oxford University Press, 1969.

Bloom, Allan. *The Closing of the American Mind*. New York: Simon and Schuster, 1987.

Bloom, Harold. *The Anxiety of Influence*. Oxford: Oxford University Press, 1973.

Bradley, A. C. *Oxford Lectures on Poetry*. Oxford: Oxford University Press, 1950.

Cervantes Saavedra, Miguel de. *Don Quixote de la Mancha*. Translated by J. M. Cohen. London: Penguin, 1950.

Cervantes Saavedra, Miguel de. *Don Quixote de la Mancha*. Translated by J. M. Cohen. London: Penguin, 1950.

Charvet, John. "Individual Identity and Social Consciousness in Rousseau's Philosophy." In *Hobbes and Rousseau*, edited by Maurice Cranston and R. S. Peters, 462-484. New York: Anchor Books, 1972.

Constant, Benjamin. *De la liberté chez les Modernes*. Edited by Marcel Gauchet. Paris: Pluriel, 1980.

───────. *Political Writings*. Translated by Biancamaria Fontana. Cambridge: Cambridge University Press, 1988.

Cranston, Maurice. *Jean-Jacques Rousseau: The Early Years*. London: Allen Lane, 1983.

Culler, Jonathan. *Theory and Criticism After Structuralism*. Ithaca, N.Y.: Cornell University Press, 1982.

De Man, Paul. *Allegories of Reading*. New Haven, Conn.: Yale University Press, 1979.

───────. "Pascal's Allegory of Persuasion." In *Allegory and Representation*, edited by Stephen Greenblatt, 1-26. Baltimore: Johns Hopkins University Press, 1981.

───────. "The Rhetoric of Temporality." In *Interpretation: Theory and Practice*, edited by Charles S. Singleton, 173-209. Baltimore: Johns Hopkins University Press, 1969.

Derrida, Jacques. *La carte postale de Socrate à Freud et au-delà*. Paris: Aubier-Flammarion, 1980.

───────. *De la grammatologie*. Paris: Editions de Minuit, 1967.

───────. *Glas*. Translated by John P. Leavey, Jr., and Richard Rand. Lincoln: University of Nebraska Press, 1990.

───────. *Marges de la philosophie*. Paris: Editions de Minuit, 1972.

───────. "La pharmacie de Platon." *Tel Quel* 32 (Winter 1968): 3-49 and 33 (Spring 1968): 18-60.

───────. *Spurs/Éperons*. Translated by Barbara Harlow. Chicago: University of Chicago Press, 1979.

Elshtain, Jean Bethke. *Public Man, Private Woman*. Princeton, N.J.: Princeton University Press, 1981.

Euben, J. Peter. *The Tragedy of Political Theory*. Princeton, N.J.: Princeton University Press, 1990.

Flathman, Richard. *The Philosophy and Politics of Freedom*. Chicago: University of Chicago Press, 1987.

Foucault, Michel. *Language, Counter-Memory, Practice.* Translated by Donald Bouchard and Sherry Simon. Ithaca, N.Y.: Cornell University Press, 1977.

―――――. *Surveiller et punir.* Paris: Gallimard, 1975.

Fowler, Alastaire. *Kinds of Literature.* Cambridge, Mass.: Harvard University Press, 1982.

Freccero, John. "Autobiography and Narrative." In *Reconstructing Individualism,* edited by Thomas C. Heller, David E. Wellbery, and Morton Sosna, 16-30. Stanford: Stanford University Press, 1986.

―――――. *Dante, the Poetics of Conversion.* Cambridge, Mass.: Harvard University Press, 1986.

Frye, Northrop. *Anatomy of Criticism: Four Essays.* Princeton, N.J.: Princeton University Press, 1957.

Gadamer, Hans-Georg. *Dialogue and Dialectic: Eight Hermeneutical Studies on Plato.* Translated by P. C. Smith. New Haven: Yale University Press, 1980.

Goldhill, Simon. *Reading Greek Tragedy.* Cambridge: Cambridge University Press, 1986.

Hartz, Louis. *The Liberal Tradition in America.* New York: Harcourt Brace, 1955.

Hegel, Georg Wilhelm Friedrich. *Lectures on Fine Arts.* Translated by T. M. Knox. 3 vols. Oxford: Oxford University Press, 1975.

―――――. *Phenomenology of Spirit.* Translated by A. V. Miller. Oxford: Oxford University Press, 1977.

―――――. *Philosophy of Right.* Translated by T. M. Knox. Oxford: Oxford University Press, 1952.

―――――. *Sämtliche Werke.* Edited by Georg Lasson and Johannes Hoffmeister. 30 vols. Leipzig: Felix Meiner, 1920-1960.

Holmes, Stephen. "Aristippus in and out of Athens." *American Political Science Review* 73 (March 1979): 113-129.

Homer. *The Iliad.* Translated by Richmond Lattimore. Chicago: University of Chicago Press, 1951.

―――――. *Odyssey.* Loeb Classical Library. 1926.

Howells, Christina. *Sartre: The Necessity of Freedom.* Cambridge: Cambridge University Press, 1988.

Hyppolite, Jean. *Genesis and Structure of Hegel's Phenomenology.* Translated by Samuel Cherniak and John Heckman. Evanston, Ill.: Northwestern University Press, 1974.

James, William. *Essays on Pragmatism*. Edited by Alburey Castell. New York: Hafner, 1951.
Jefferson, Thomas. *Jefferson's Writings*. Edited by Merrill D. Peterson. New York: Library of America, 1984.
Kateb, George. *Hannah Arendt: Politics, Conscience, Evil*. Oxford: Martin Robertson, 1983.
Kerr, Walter. *Tragedy and Comedy*. London: Bodley Head, 1967.
Kundera, Milan. *The Book of Laughter and Forgetting*. Translated by Michael Henry Heim. London: Penguin, 1978.
MacCallum, Gerald C., Jr. "Negative and Positive Freedom." *Philosophical Review* 76 (July 1976): 312-335.
MacIntyre, Alasdair. *Whose Justice? Which Rationality?* Notre Dame, Ind.: University of Notre Dame Press, 1988.
McWilliams, Wilson Carey. *The Idea of Fraternity in America*. Berkeley and Los Angeles: University of California Press, 1973.
Madison, James, Hamilton, Alexander, and Jay, John. *The Federalist Papers*. Edited by Isaac Kramnick. London: Penguin, 1987.
Marks, Elaine, and Isabelle de Courtivron, eds. *New French Feminisms*. Amherst: University of Massachusetts Press, 1980.
Marx, Karl. *Early Writings*. Translated by Tom Bottomore. London: C. Watts, 1963.
_____. *Historisch-kritische Gesamtausgabe*. Edited by David Rjazanov, et. al. 13 vols. Berlin: Marx-Engels Verlag, 1932.
_____. *Selected Writings*. Translated by David McLellan. Oxford: Oxford University Press, 1977.
Nietzsche, Friedrich. *Beyond Good and Evil*. Translated by Walter Kaufmann. New York: Vintage, 1969.
_____. *Genealogy of Morals*. Translated by Walter Kaufmann. New York: Vintage, 1958.
_____. *Nietzsche Werke*. Edited by Giorgio Colli and Mazzino Montinari. 8 vols. Berlin: Walter de Gruyter Verlag, 1972.
Norris, Christopher. *Contest of Faculties*. London: Methuen, 1985.
Nussbaum, Martha. *The Fragility of Goodness*. Cambridge: Cambridge University Press, 1986.
Pangle, Thomas. *The Spirit of Modern Republicanism*. Chicago: University of Chicago Press, 1988.
Pitkin, Hanna. "Are Freedom and Liberty Twins?" *Political Theory* 16 (November 1988): 523-553.

_____. "On Relating Private and Public." *Political Theory* 9 (August 1981): 331-338.

Plato, *The Collected Dialogues of Plato*. Edited by Edith Hamilton and Huntington Cairns. Translated by Hamilton, Cairns et. al. Princeton, N.J.: Princeton University Press, 1961.

_____. *Plato*. 12 vols. Loeb Classical Library. 1914-1926.

_____. *The Republic*. Translated by Raymond Larson. Arlington Heights, Ill.: Harlan Davidson, 1979.

Pocock, J.G.A. *The Machiavellian Moment: Florentine Political Thought and the Atlantic Republican Tradition*. Princeton, N.J.: Princeton University Press, 1975.

Poulet, Georges. *Studies in Human Time*. Translated by Elliott Coleman. Baltimore: Johns Hopkins University Press, 1956.

Rorty, Richard. *Consequence of Pragmatism*. Minneapolis: University of Minnesota Press, 1982.

_____. *Contingency, Irony and Solidarity*. Cambridge: Cambridge University Press, 1989.

_____. *Philosophy and the Mirror of Nature*. Princeton, N.J.: Princeton University Press, 1979.

_____. "That Old Time Philosophy," *New Republic* 198 (April 1988): 28-33.

_____. "The Priority of Democracy to Philosophy." In *The Virginia Statute for Religious Freedom: Its Evolution and Consequences*, edited by Merrill D. Peterson and Robert C. Vaughan, 257-282. Cambridge: Cambridge University Press, 1988.

_____. "Thugs and Theorists." *Political Theory* 15 (November 1987): 564-573.

_____. "Unger, Castoriadis, and the Romance of a National Future." *Northwestern University Law Review* 82 (Winter 1988): 343-362.

Rousseau, Jean-Jacques. "De l'imitation théâtrale." In *Oeuvres*, vol. 2, 2-20. Paris: Armand-Aubrée, 1832.

_____. *The First and Second Discourses*. Translated by Judith Masters and Roger Masters. New York: St. Martin's Press, 1968.

_____. *Julie: ou La Nouvelle Héloïse*. Paris: Garnier, 1967.

_____. *Oeuvres complètes*. Edited by Bernard Gagnebin and Marcel Raymond. 4 vols. Paris: Gallimard, 1964.

_____. *Politics and the Arts*. Translated by Allan Bloom. Ithaca, N.Y.: Cornell University Press, 1960.

―――――. *The Social Contract*. Translated by Maurice Cranston. London: Penguin, 1968.
Sartre, Jean-Paul. *Being and Nothingness*. Translated by Hazel E. Barnes. New York: Washington Square Press, 1966.
―――――. *Between Existentialism and Marxism*. Translated by John Mathews. New York: Pantheon, 1974.
―――――. *Qu'est-ce que la littérature?* Paris: Gallimard, 1949.
―――――. *L'Etre et le néant*. Paris: Gallimard, 1943.
―――――. *Existentialism and Human Emotions*. Translated and edited by Bernard Frechtman. New York: Philosophical Library Press, 1957.
―――――. *L'Existentialism est un humanisme*. Paris: Nagel, 1946.
―――――. *L'Idiot de la famille*. 4 vols. Paris: Gallimard, 1971-1974.
―――――. *Les Mains sales*. Paris: Gallimard, 1948.
―――――. *La Nausée*. In *Oeuvres romanesques*, edited by Michel Contat and Michel Rybalka. Paris: Gallimard, 1981.
―――――. *Saint Genet, comédien et martyr*. Paris: Gallimard, 1952.
―――――. *Situations 3*. Paris: Gallimard, 1949.
―――――. *Un Théâtre de situations*. Edited by Michel Contat and Michel Rybalka. Paris: Gallimard, 1973.
Saxonhouse, Arlene. "Comedy in *Callipolis*: Animal Imagery in the *Republic*." *American Political Science Review* 72 (September 1978): 888-901.
Sayers, Dorothy. *Introductory Papers on Dante*. Oxford: Oxford University Press, 1956.
Schwartz, Joel. *The Sexual Politics of Jean-Jacques Rousseau*. Chicago: University of Chicago Press, 1984.
Segal, Charles. *Tragedy and Civilization*. Cambridge, Mass.: Harvard University Press, 1981.
Seidentop, L. A. "Two Liberal Traditions." In *The Idea of Freedom*, edited by Alan Ryan, 153-174. Oxford: Oxford University Press, 1979.
Shapiro, Gary. *Nietzschean Narratives*. Bloomington: Indiana University Press, 1989.
Shklar, Judith. *Men and Citizens*. Cambridge: Cambridge University Press, 1969.
Skinner, Quentin. "The Idea of Negative Liberty." In *Philosophy in History*, edited by Quentin Skinner, Richard Rorty, and Jerome B. Schneewind, 193-224. Cambridge: Cambridge University Press, 1984.
Solomon, Robert. *In the Spirit of Hegel*. Oxford: Oxford University Press, 1983.

Selected Bibliography

Sophocles, *Antigone*. In *Sophocles I*, translated by Elizabeth Wyckoff. Chicago: University of Chicago Press, 1954.
Staël, Germaine de. *De l'allemagne*. Edited by Jean de Pange. 5 vols. Paris: Librairie Hachette, 1959.
Starobinski, Jean. *L'Oeil vivant*. Paris: Gallimard, 1961.
Taylor, Charles. "What's Wrong with Negative Liberty?" In *The Idea of Freedom*, edited by Alan Ryan, 175-194. Oxford: Oxford University Press, 1979.
Taylor, Mark C. *Altarity*. Chicago: University of Chicago Press, 1987.
_____. *Tears*. Albany: State University of New York Press, 1990.
Tocqueville, Alexis de. *Democracy in America*. Edited by J. P. Mayer. Translated by George Lawrence. New York: Doubleday, 1969.
_____. *Oeuvres complètes*. Edited by J. P. Mayer. 12 vols. Paris: Librairie de Medicis, 1951-1964.
Vernant, Jean-Pierre, and Vidal-Naquet, Pierre. *Mythe et tragédie en Grèce ancienne*. Paris: Maspero, 1972.
Voegelin, Eric. *Plato*. Baton Rouge: Louisiana State University Press, 1960.
Warnock, Mary. *Existentialism*. Oxford: Oxford University Press, 1970.
Weber, Max. *From Max Weber*. Translated by H. H. Gerth and C. Wright Mills. Oxford: Oxford University Press, 1956.
_____. *Max Weber: Soziologie, Weltgeschichtliche Analysen, Politik*. Edited by Johannes Winckelmann. Stuttgart: Alfred Kröner, 1964.
_____. *Wirtschaft und Gesellschaft: Grundriss der Verstehenden Soziologie*. Edited by Johannes Winckelmann. 2 vols. Tübingen: J.C.B. Mohr, 1956.
White, Hayden. *Metahistory*. Baltimore: Johns Hopkins University Press, 1973.
Wood, Gordon S. *The Creation of the American Republic 1776-1787*. Chapel Hill: University of North Carolina Press, 1969.
Zeitlin, Froma. "Playing the 'Other.'" *Representations* 11 (Summer 1985): 63-94.

About the Book and Author

To do political theory is to tell a story about human beings and their communities. In this witty and elegant book, Michael Brint provides a brilliant reading of some of the greatest stories told in the history of Western political theory. The unifying theme is the issue of differences and the conflicts they generate. Brint's targets are those thinkers, classical and contemporary, who would deny the reality of difference and the necessarily tragic element inherent in human political society.

There are many ways to deny or cover up the tragic element in human affairs, including appeals to dialectics, to irony, and to an ineffable *différance*. But against ironists, deconstructionists, and all the others, Brint urges that ethical differences should be taken literally, with the respect necessary to come to terms with the conflicts that inevitably arise in real-life pluralistic communities.

Always graceful and entertaining, *Tragedy and Denial* makes a significant contribution to our understanding of historical and contemporary political thought. It is essential reading for anyone who would take part in this continuing conversation.

Michael Brint is assistant professor of government and foreign affairs at the University of Virginia.

Index

Achilleus, 15-17, 29, 133
Aeschylus, 28, 168
Alighieri, Dante, 18, 87-88, 107(n2)
Amour de soi, 48, 51-52, 93
Amour propre, 51-52, 55-56, 59-60, 82-83, 93-94, 120
Alterity, 166-167
Antigone (Sophocles), 11, 30, 158-168, *passim* 157-167
Antitragedy, 3-7, 16, 27, 30, 36-37
Arendt, Hannah, 131-133, 138-142, 145, 147, 148, 149, 151
  on freedom (political), 135, 137
  on liberty (individual), 136
Aristotle, 4, 33, 46, 54, 141, 142, 157
Augustine, St., 48

Bakhtin, Mikhail, 56
Ball, Terence, 152(n2)
Barber, Benjamin, 61(n4), 85(n9), 152(n2)
Berlin, Isaiah, 62(n18), 68, 103-106, 147, 149
Bloom, Allan, 62(n7), 148, 154(n28)
Bloom, Harold, 134
Bradley, A. C., 1, 69, 84

Cabell, Joseph C., 152(n4)
Cervantes, Miguel Saavedra de, 6, 67-68, 152
Charvet, John, 62(n13)
Comedy, 5, 7, 16, 19, 37, 68, 87, 91, 100, 109-111, 144, 148, 158-60
  See also under Hegel, G.W.F.
Constant, Benjamin, 69-84, 139-140, 142
Courtivron, Isabelle de, 168(n8)
Cranston, Maurice, 61(n2)
Culler, Jonathan, 168(n8)

Deconstruction, 3, 125-126, 161, 162, 163
  See also Derrida, Jacques
De Man, Paul, 38(nn 5, 10), 59, 62(n10)
Derrida, Jacques, 7, 9, 11, 50, 111, 121-126, 144, 157, 162, 163, 165
Desan, Wilfrid, 127(n12)
Dewey, John, 9, 143
Dostoevsky, Fyodor, 120

Elshtain, Jean Bethke, 127(n10)

Faust (Goethe), 53, 120
Fichte, Johann Gottlieb, 42, 123
Flathman, Richard, 154(n32)
Flaubert, Gustave, 128(n21)
Forman, Janis, 61(n4)
Foucault, Michel, 23, 109-111, 127(nn2-3, 5-7), 144, 145
Fowler, Alastaire, 11(n2)
Freccero, John, 38(n9), 62(n10)
Freedom (political), 6, 68-71, 78, 92, 98, 100, 135-137, 142, 148-151, 158
  See also Republicanism; under

179

Hegel, G.W.F.; Rorty, Richard; Rousseau, Jean-Jacques
Frye, Northrop, 107(n3)

Gadamer, Hans-Georg, 62(n8)
Gender differentiation, 4-5, 31, 33, 60, 159, 165-167
Gide, Andre, 115
Goldhill, Simon, 167(n3)

Hartz, Louis, 152(n2)
Hegel, Georg Wilhelm Friedrich, 7, 8, 11, 50, 61, 62(n14), 69, 84, (ch. 4), 124-126, 135, 136, 144, 153(n5), 157-164
and comedy, 87, 91, 100, 109, 114-121
on freedom (political), 92, 98, 100
on liberty (individual), 91-94, 98
Hektor, 18, 29-30, 34
Holmes, Stephen, 85(n8)
Homer, 18, 21-24, 29-30, 34
Howells, Christina, 128(n13)
Humboldt, Wilhelm von, 76
Husserl, Edmund, 121, 124
Hyppolite, Jean, 108(n13)

Irony, 3-4, 7, 20, 35-37, 114, 145, 147, 151, 157, 162-163
See also Deconstruction;Satire

James, William, 145-146, 149
Jefferson, Thomas, 131, 137, 144, 151

Kant, Immanuel, 113, 115, 123, 146-147
Kateb, George, 154(n19)
Kercheval, Samuel, 152(n4)
Kerr, Walter, 62(n9)
Kierkegaard, Søren, 115-116
Kundera, Milan, 106

Liberalism, 70, 85(n8), 99-100, 113, 134, 137, 143, 145-147, 151
Liberty (individual), (ch. 3), 91-94, 98, 100, 105, 135-137, 140, 141, 142, 145, 149, 150, 151
See also under Arendt, Hannah; Hegel, G.W.F.; Rorty, Richard

MacCallum, Gerald C., Jr., 84(n2)
MacIntyre, Alasdair, 168(n13)
McWilliams, Wilson Carey, 152(n2)
Machiavelli, Niccolò, 150
Marivaux, Pierre de Chamblain de, 41
Marks, Elaine, 168(n8)
Marx, Karl, 86(n13), 105-106
Metaphor, 2, 10, 26, 28, 34, 45, 54, 59-60, 112-113, 123, 132, 134-135, 140, 147-149
Mill, John Stuart, 145, 146, 147

Nabokov, Vladimir, 144
Narcisse (Rousseau), 5, 41-44, 58
Nietzsche, Friedrich, 62(n11), 109-111, 121, 124, 126, 144, 145, 148, 165, 168(n8)
Norris, Christopher, 147
Nussbaum, Martha, 159-160

Orwell, George, 144
Other, 46, 58, 93, 96, 110, 116-118, 123, 136, 157
as dialectical, 88-91, 160
as different, 163-168
as ineffable, 8-11, 125-126, 144, 161-163
Ovid, 42

Pangle, Thomas, 152(n2)
Pitkin, Hanna, 153(n10), 154(nn 21, 30)

Index

Plato, 3, (ch. 1), 44-46, 59
Pluralism, 131, 147, 150, 151, 167
Pocock, J.G.A., 152(n2)
Political culture, 1, 150, 151, 160
Political participation.
  See Freedom (political)
Postmodern, 109, 145, 161
  See Also Deconstruction; Derrida, Jacques; Foucault, Michel; Nietzsche, Friedrich; Sartre, Jean-Paul
Poulet, George, 53

Rawls, John, 146
Republic (Plato), 3, 16, 20-26, 32, 37, 44-45
Republicanism, 131, 137, 152(n2)
Romance, 9-10
  See also under Rorty, Richard
Rorty, Richard, 7, 9-10, 131
  on freedom (political), 151
  on liberty (individual), 145-147, 149
  and romance, 132-135, 143-144
Rousseau, Jean-Jacques, 5-7, (ch. 2), 69-84, 91-96, 98, 100, 103, 119, 168(n8)
  on freedom (political), 138-139, 140, 142
Royer-Collard, Pierre, 153(n16)

Sartre, Jean-Paul, 7-8, 111, 136, 144
  and satire, 112-121
Satire, 3, 9, 68, 109, 126
  See also under Sartre, Jean-Paul
Saxonhouse, Arlene, 39 (n12)
Sayers, Dorothy, 107(n1)
Schwartz, Joel, 61(n3)
Segal, Charles, 168(n12)

Seidentop, L. A., 85(n8), 154(n32)
Shapiro, Gary, 127(n8)
Shklar, Judith, 85(n9)
Skinner, Quentin, 150
Social Contract, The (Rousseau), 54, 71-72, 76, 78, 80, 83, 85(n10)
Socrates, 3, 5-7 (ch. 1), 44-45, 59-60
Solomon, Robert, 91
Sophocles, 10, 30, 157, 158, 159, 163, 167
Staël, Germaine de, 3, 71, 76
Starobinski, Jean, 62(n9)
Storytelling, political theory as, 1, 133
Swift, Jonathan, 70

Taylor, Charles, 84(n2), 154(n24)
Taylor, Mark C., 154(n3), 161
Thuycidides, 36
Tocqueville, Alexis de, 137, 148, 150
Tolstoy, Leo, 133
Tragedy, 1, 2, 3, 5, 7, 69, 84, 89-91, 115, 151, 159-160

Vernant, Jean-Pierre, 11(n6)
Vidal-Naquet, Pierre, 11(n6)
Voegelin, Eric, 38 (n6)
Voltaire, Jean François Marie Arouet de, 41

Warnock, Mary, 128(n23)
Weber, Max, 80, 153(n7)
White, Hayden, 127(n1)
Wittgenstein, Ludwig, 135, 144
Wood, Gordon S., 152(n7)

Zeitlin, Froma, 39 (n11)